Building Proficiency for World Language Learners

This innovative book offers over 100 engaging and effective activities that busy teachers can use to help students become confident, comfortable, and proficient learners, acquirers, and communicators in new languages. Many activities can be adapted to different languages and levels in secondary-level language courses.

Klimas provides readers with ready-to-use templates, editable posters, as well as multimodal communicative activities such as games, storytelling exercises, ideas for centers, and more. There are also pair work and speaking, listening, and reading, as well as drama and video activities to build fluency and encourage risk-taking in the target language.

Chock full of low-prep, engaging ideas, *Building Proficiency for World Language Learners* is an essential tool for world language and ESL teachers.

Janina Klimas is a teacher, linguist, and author. She has taught languages for over 25 years on three different continents and speaks six languages to various levels of fluency. She has a BA in Theater Arts and Foreign Languages and an MA in the Teaching of Languages. She is certified to teach Spanish, English, drama, speech, grades K-8, social studies, gifted education, language immersion, and reading, and has led workshops for language teachers.

Also Available from Routledge Eye On Education
(www.routledge.com/eyeoneducation)

Differentiated Instruction: A Guide for World Language Teachers
Deborah Blaz

Sentence Strategies for Multilingual Learners: Advancing Academic Literacy through Combinations
Nell Scharff Panero and Joanna Yip

Teaching World Languages with the Five Senses: Practical Strategies and Ideas for Hands-On Learning
Elizabeth Porter

Going Global in the World Language Classroom: Ideas, Strategies, and Resources for Teaching and Learning With the World
Erin Austin

Sparking Creativity in the World Language Classroom: Strategies and Ideas to Build Your Students' Language Skills
Deborah Blaz and Tom Alsop

The Antiracist World Language Classroom
Krishauna Hines-Gaither and Cécile Accilien

Building Proficiency for World Language Learners

100+ High-Interest Activities

Janina Klimas

Routledge
Taylor & Francis Group
NEW YORK AND LONDON

First published 2024
by Routledge
605 Third Avenue, New York, NY 10158

and by Routledge
4 Park Square, Milton Park, Abingdon, Oxon, OX14 4RN

Routledge is an imprint of the Taylor & Francis Group, an informa business

© 2024 Janina Klimas

The right of Janina Klimas to be identified as author of this work has been asserted in accordance with sections 77 and 78 of the Copyright, Designs and Patents Act 1988.

All rights reserved. The purchase of this copyright material confers the right on the purchasing institution to photocopy or download pages which bear a copyright line at the bottom of the page. No other parts of this book may be reprinted or reproduced or utilised in any form or by any electronic, mechanical, or other means, now known or hereafter invented, including photocopying and recording, or in any information storage or retrieval system, without permission in writing from the publishers.

Trademark notice: Product or corporate names may be trademarks or registered trademarks, and are used only for identification and explanation without intent to infringe.

ISBN: 9781032622026 (hbk)
ISBN: 9781032615912 (pbk)
ISBN: 9781032622507 (ebk)

DOI: 10.4324/9781032622507

Typeset in Palatino
by codeMantra

Access the Support Material: www.routledge.com/9781032615912

Contents

Meet the Author x
Introduction xi

SECTION 1

1   **The Proficiency-Oriented Language Classroom** 2

SECTION 2

2   **Lesson Planning and Starting the Year** 20

SECTION 3

3   **Low- and No-Prep Games** 42
   Charades 43
   Pictionary Three Ways 43
   Instant Games: Post-its and Index Cards 44
   Scattergories/Categories 46
   CharPictionary/Taboo 48
   Bingo 49
   Races 52
   Two (or Three) Truths and a Lie 52
   Buzzers, Bells, Balls, and Other Fun Things 53
   Flashcards and Card Games 54
   Tasks 56
   The Can-Do Game 59
   Tic-Tac-Toe Four Ways 60
   Hangman 62

vi ◆ Contents

SECTION 4

4   Student-Centered Communicative Activities **66**
Feelings/Emotions 66
Family 67
Weather and Seasons 69
Home 71
Shopping 72
Clothing 74
Menus and Restaurants 76
The Time 77
Mini Tasks 78
Short Simulations and Dramatizations 80
Fake Texts 80
Doodles, Sketches, Drawings, and Short Writing
Google Translate and Artificial Intelligence 86

5   Communicative and Research Projects **88**
Cultural Research Projects 88
High-Interest Compare and Contrast 91
Argue and Persuade 91
Travel 96
Travel Realia 97
Real-Life Task Practice 99
More Engaging Projects 102

SECTION 5

6   Reading **104**
Summaries 107
Interesting Scenes 108
Mark up Text and Highlight 108
Questions 109
Read with Others 109
SQ3R 110
My Character 111
History 112

Contents ◆ vii

Magazines 113
Audiobooks 113
Reading Journals 113
Uncomfortable Conversations 114
What Happened in the Story? 115
5 W's Book Summary 116
The Hand Reading Summary 116
Readlang Browser Extension 117

7 Pair Work and Speaking **118**
Research-Based Interviews 118
More Activities with Questions and Answers 119
Guest Speakers and Special Person Interviews 123
Language Experience Approach 128
Surveys 128
Show and Tell 130
Did You Do It? 130
Transform Textbook Activities into Pair Work 131
Chat Mats 131
Descriptions 133
Presentations/Speaking Activities 135
Dice 136
M.A.S.H. 136
Review Project 137
Slides 142
Recordings 143
Scavenger/Treasure Hunt 144
Guess Who? 144
Debate 146
Speed Dating 147
Chat in Class 148
More Activities with Cards 151

8 Grammar, Listening, and Writing **153**
Practical Ways to Introduce Students to Grammar in
Context 154
Is it True? 157

viii ◆ Contents

Grammar Matching and Mastery Games 158
Three in a Row 165
Affirmations 166
Corner Game 166
Listening Labs 168
Ping-Pong Listening 168
YouTube Transcripts/Grammar in Context. 168
Timed Writing 169
Poems 171
Emails and Letters. 172
Ranking Activities. 172
Graphic Organizers. 172
Comics. 173
100-Word Writing Prompts 173

9 **Culture** **177**
Music. 179
Blogs and Realia. 181
Literature, Film, and Art. 182
Exercise 182
Community Service. 183
Travel Abroad. 183
Putting it All Together. 184

10 **Centers, Stations, and Choices.** **186**
Centers and Stations 186
Choices 188
Game Night (or Day) 189

11 **Video and Drama Activities** **190**
Get the Part. 190
Rehearsing for a Role 191
Reader's Theater 191
Complaints. 192
Subtitles. 193
Sound Effects 193
Narration. 194
Word Story 195

Contents ◆ ix

Screenplay..196
Set and Costume Design............................196
Perform an Extended Play..........................197
Fairy Tale Trial.....................................197
Exchange Students.................................198
Hot Seat..199
Special Event.......................................201
More Dialogues, Skits, Simulations, and Dramatizations...201
Movie Talk...203
Movie Reviews......................................204
Movie Night..204
Video Diaries.......................................205
Short-Form Videos..................................205
Video Prompts for Language Learners...............205
More Prompts.......................................207
Reading Reaction...................................208
Test Review...209
Puppet Shows......................................209

SECTION 6

12 Assessments.......................................212
Summative and Proficiency Assessments.............213
Quick Check-ins.....................................214
Formative Assessments in Your Classroom...........216

SECTION 7

13 Professional Development........................228
Conferences and Social Media.......................228
Fill Your Cup.......................................229
Not-Do List...229
Oxygen Mask.......................................230
Make Your Life Easier Next Year....................230
Engaging in Activities that You Enjoy...............230
Graduate Work......................................231
Language Proficiency...............................231
Don't Reinvent the Wheel, and Find Your Peeps........236

Meet the Author

Janina Klimas will show you how to learn a language. She has taught languages for over 25 years on three different continents. She has studied in her native United States, France, and Spain, and spent almost a decade teaching languages in Asia.

Janina has a BA in Theater Arts and Foreign Languages, and an MA in the Teaching of Languages. She is certified to teach Spanish, English, ESL, gifted and talented education, drama, speech, language immersion, social studies, and reading. She has led workshops for language teachers online, at the BETT Show in London, the annual ACTFL convention, Language Show Live in London, the Polyglot Conference, the annual AATSP conference, and at schools in Europe and the US. Janina has also contributed to *The Language Educator, Fluent in Three Months*, and has been featured on several podcasts such as Marc Guberti's Breakthrough Success, and *NYT* bestselling author Chris Guillebeau's Side Hustle School podcast.

Introduction

When I first started teaching languages in the mid-1990s, I had no intention of doing so long-term. I came to the profession with a BA in theater arts and foreign languages, unsure if teaching was the right career path for me. But teaching was an opportunity that offered the possibility of travel, and the work seemed creative and rewarding.

The reality of teaching languages was all of that and more. This vocation does provide the possibility of travel for anyone willing to work abroad, even for a short period of time, and the work is indeed creative. We can draw so much from the world around us to bring language and culture into our classrooms from all over the world. The work is also incredibly rewarding. We can give students experiences that allow them to communicate with people who speak languages other than their own in our classes.

Anyone who aspires to be a teacher should also have knowledge of the reality of what it is like to be a teacher in many parts of the world. It is said that teachers make more decisions than air traffic controllers—considered one of the most stressful jobs in existence. In the United States, many teachers leave within five years of entering the profession. Each year, half a million teachers either move or leave their occupation, costing the United States up to 2.2 billion dollars (O'Meara).

There are even more statistics to consider. According to an article published in *The Atlantic* (Friedman), more than 90 percent of schools in our country offer foreign languages, but less than 1 percent of Americans are proficient in a language studied in a classroom in the U.S.

We also have standards to meet. Many of our programs require us to bring students from one specific point to another. The reality is that while we have those standards (ours and others'), we aren't always given the tools we need to reach them. This might include rigid daily plans that don't take into account the different people within a group we teach, inadequate (or no) materials or technology, and unmotivated students who are either there because it is required or not realistic about the time and effort needed to reach their desired goals. How do we do so much with so little?

I love language teachers. While I am obviously biased, they are undeniably interesting. Some of us come from other countries, and some of us grew up in families with multiple cultures. Many language teachers fell in love with languages after starting them at school, but regardless of how we got started, we share one commonality: our desire to give students all of the wonderful benefits of a second language. We want to help people have more work and social opportunities, more money in retirement, as well as the research-based health benefits of exposure to more than one language.

In this book, we'll explore how you can have a proficiency-oriented language classroom that guides learners to real-world language proficiency in a sustainable way which allows us busy teachers to still have a life.

As your colleague, I would like to start with a couple of notes. First, we are all at different points in our different journeys. Please know that these activities may have the professor's mistake, where something was not explained adequately enough due to assuming everyone had enough context or details. Conversely, it also may feel like the obvious was pointed out. Please know it is not my intention to not provide sufficient explanation or insult your expertise. Reach out with questions you might have and skip over what isn't relevant for you.

References

O'Meara, James. "Teacher Attrition Key to Global Education Targets." *University World News*, 28 November 2014, www.universityworldnews.com/post.php?story=201411261729478

67#:~:text=However%2C%20that%20ignores%20the%20very, goal%20to%20red.

Friedman, Amelia. "America's Lacking Language Skills." *The Atlantic*, 11 May 2015, www.theatlantic.com/education/archive/2015/05/ filling-americas-language-education-potholes/392876.

SECTION 1

Members understand that proficiency focuses on what people can do with the language and not what they can't do.

1

The Proficiency-Oriented Language Classroom

While it isn't critical for us to know exactly how a car works in order to get to the places we need to go, it certainly helps. This knowledge also helps us make smart decisions with regard to how we use our vehicles and how we maintain them. For me, learning and often checking in with the research on second language acquisition has been instrumental in getting learners proficient in other languages.

There is much research done on how people learn languages, and the majority of it is excellent and useful. With that said, I like to keep things simple. I also believe that the more concise and easier someone can make a concept, the more they know what they're talking about. While I say this without disrespect to any researchers out there, I think there is no better person to present the most important things anybody who is interested in learning and teaching languages needs to know than Dr. Steven Krashen.

Krashen's theory of second language acquisition consists of five main hypotheses:

- ◆ the Acquisition-Learning hypothesis
- ◆ the Monitor hypothesis
- ◆ the Natural Order hypothesis

DOI: 10.4324/9781032622507-2

- ◆ the Input hypothesis
- ◆ the Affective Filter hypothesis.

Here's my cheat sheet on Krashen's theories:

Acquisition-Learning

Acquisition is natural. Learning is intentional and more artificial. Think about the way you learned your own language as a child. You were immersed in messages. You were read to. You watched television. You listened to songs. You read.

With learning, think about some of the formal instruction you had in school—for example, what a noun or an adverb is. Instruction on parts of speech and grammar exercises are examples of formal language instruction that many of us have experienced.

Monitor

This is the practical result of the language learned. It discusses how learners monitor what they have learned and acquired in the new language. For example, some over-monitor and as a result are overly measured in their language use, ultimately at the expense of communication. Some under-monitor at the expense of accuracy. Ideal learners remain aware enough to monitor their use in the right balance to allow for continued progress yet don't let mistakes halt their progress.

Natural Order

As Krashen says, "For a given language, some grammatical structures tend to be acquired early, while others late." I like to use the example of children again. Think about some of the simple things they say when they're first learning to speak. They're choppy and rough. But by the time someone graduates from college, their language is sophisticated and polished relative to a small child, and they have ease of expression. While this natural order seems to be similar among languages and learner profiles, grammar does not need to be learned in a specific sequence.

Input

In order to keep skills growing in a language, we need comprehensible input. This is language that can be understood, with some new things in there that allow for problem solving, thinking, and acquiring new structures. They allow learners to work on language that is slightly more difficult—just above their level of language—incorporating that into what is already known.

Affective Filter

This can have a huge impact on how quickly a language is learned/acquired. Languages can be pretty scary. Does the learner have an outgoing personality? Are they extroverts? Are they willing to put themselves out there, or are they perfectionists, measured with their communication?

What this means for the learners we're guiding:

◆ **Acquisition:** Speak early on. It's ideal. It can also be perfectly tailored and personalized. Get input and produce output. This helps learners test themselves and refine constantly as they go.

◆ **Learning:** Don't worry about all the rules. Invest time in one of the three modes of communication: interpretive, interpersonal, or presentational (ACTFL). When learners start understanding the rules and seeing patterns without explanations, that's the perfect time to learn the rules. That's how we learned our first language. We didn't learn nouns by understanding that they were a person, place, thing, or idea. We learned the word first, then learned what part of speech they were later.

The Proficiency-Oriented Language Classroom ◆ 5

◆ **Monitor (input hypothesis):** Refinement of grammar and structures will come with time. Focus on communicating. I don't think it's a bad thing to invest time in the teaching of grammar. We learn a lot of grammar and structure in context, saving hours and hours of time on difficult exercises that won't make better speakers. Listening to people, reading, and then having some context to use that language is the greatest way to master language and structures—not explanations.

◆ **Natural order:** We all tend to go through the same phases. For example, intermediate/B-level speakers create with language by speaking in sentences. Their grammar is understandable though a bit choppy. With time comes refinement. The more time invested in input and practice—that natural, communicative input—the more skills will improve.

◆ **Affective filter:** We're not all extroverts. With that said, remember that the more one puts themselves out there, the better their skills will become, and more quickly.

Don't worry about perfection. Get talking. If that means learners talking to themselves for a long time before feeling comfortable talking to somebody else, do it. Most importantly—be kind. Have the kind of compassion we'd have for a child learning a language. It can be difficult to be out there. Remember that!

If an activity or assessment sets unrealistic expectations for the learners or does not respect the proficiency level of the learner and provide comprehensible input, problem-solving opportunities to build proficiency, and opportunities to learn and acquire language, it isn't beneficial. Don't feel compelled to do every activity in a textbook. The sum of these exercises does not equal language proficiency. While so many provide rich input opportunities and valuable exercises to develop knowledge, their completion does not guarantee that the learner will attain specific proficiency targets. If an assessment does not reflect a real-world task, it may not be beneficial without some adjustments.

I also believe that the combination of acquisition and learning is the perfect marriage. This is how learners can make fast and consistent progress. Polyglots do this beautifully, using comprehensible input with deliberate learning activities to make fast progress while respecting their level as they build competence. They know they'll make errors and mistakes and that communication is key.

Language Learning + Acquisition = The Perfect Marriage

I have long been obsessed with the word *fluency*. As a learner, I was acutely aware when I wasn't fluent, yet I could not accept that it was a binary concept. The names for courses (i.e., beginner, intermediate, advanced) all seemed relative to me. They didn't help me understand what this meant in real-life terms. As a teacher and learner, this knowledge has been invaluable.

The Proficiency-Oriented Language Classroom

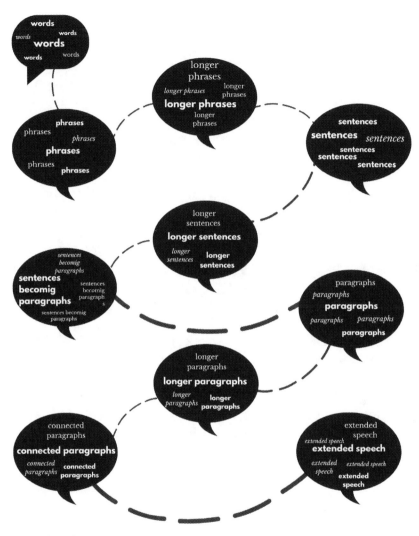

The Path to Fluency

What Is Fluent?

The bubble that talks about words and sentences becoming paragraphs is approximately the B1 or the ACTFL intermediate high. A lot of people who study a foreign language at university reach this level. It's a decent and respectable level of fluency. If you want to work professionally in a country, you need to be up toward those connected paragraphs in extended speech. However, it all counts. You don't have to be fluent to be a successful language learner. Aim for progress, not perfection.

The majority of secondary school programs operate in the Novice/A and Intermediate/B levels. While there are native speakers well into the advanced range, many school courses are often targeted to these pre-paragraph bubbles.

How Long Does it Take?

Different categories of languages take different amounts of time to learn. Languages that are close to English—think neighbors of England—are in Category I. Languages that are much more difficult and far away from England—think Korean, Japanese—take three to four times as long to reach the same level of fluency. Factor that into expectations and timelines for reaching goals. What is a reasonable level of fluency and real-world proficiency given the time students spend in the target language in your program?

See these statistics based on the Foreign Service Institute's Research on how long it takes to learn different languages in their programs to train State Department employees for life abroad.

Learning Languages: How Long Does It Take?

Category I Languages
24-30 weeks
(600-750 class hours)
Languages similar to English: Danish, Dutch, Italian, Norwegian, Romanian, Spanish (24 weeks). French (30 weeks).

Category II Languages:
Approximately 36 weeks
(900 class hours)
German, Haitian Creole, Indonesian, Malay, Swahili

Category III Languages:
Approximately 44 weeks (1100 class hours)
"Hard languages" - Languages with significant linguistic and/or cultural differences from English. This list is not exhaustive.
Albanian, Armenian, Amharic, Azerbaijani, Bengali, Bulgarian, Burmese, Czech, Dari, Estonian, Farsi, Finnish, Georgian, Greek, Hebrew, Hindi, Hungarian, Icelandic, Kazakh, Khmer, Kurdish, Kyrgyz, Lao, Latvian, Lithuanian, Macedonian, Mongolian, Nepali, Polish, Russian, Serbo-Croatian, Sinhala, Slovak, Slovenian, Somali, Tagalog, Tajiki, Tamil, Telugu, Thai, Tibetan, Turkish, Turkmen, Ukranian, Urdu, Uzbek, Vietnamese

Category IV Languages:
88 weeks
(2200 class hours)
"Super-hard languages" - Languages which are exceptionally difficult for native English speakers-Mandarin, Japanese, Korean, Arabic and Cantonese.

Source: Foreign Service Institute - United States Department of State

How Long Does It Take?

The truth is that classrooms will likely look very different from this. Some students will want to learn new languages and will someday put forth the same type of effort we see in polyglots and aspiring diplomats at some point in their lives. However, the current reality is often different. There are short amounts of time to work with our students and a lot of language to be acquired and learned. The games and activities shared here are meant to make that journey smoother and more enjoyable for students and teachers.

Here is a summary of the essentials for learning and acquiring languages in a world language classroom.

Checklist for a Proficiency-Oriented Language Class

Members understand that proficiency focuses on what people **can** do with the language and not what they **can't** do.

 The teacher uses the target language as a vehicle of instruction and communication.

 Members feel comfortable risk-taking in the target language.

 Communication is the main focus of class.

 Students and teachers have awareness of and access to proficiency-oriented assessments and use them regularly.

 The majority of class time is spent doing activities that build communicative skills. Communicative activities that involve speaking, listening, reading, writing and culture are used to build fluency in each class.

 Members understand that errors are natural on the road to fluency. Accuracy comes later.

✓ abcde
✗ adceb

Checklist for a Proficiency-Oriented Classroom

The Proficiency-Oriented Language Classroom ♦ 11

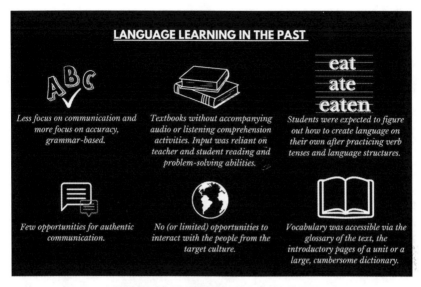

Language Learning in the Past v. the Present

The activities shared in this book are aligned with this research. Most provide learners with opportunities to both acquire and learn language. While there is space for the traditional, rote activities and assessments many of us have experienced as both learners and teachers, the proficiency-oriented classroom recognizes that skills come with time engaged in experiences

12 ◆ The Proficiency-Oriented Language Classroom

with languages. The games are meant to lower anxiety and help learners transform what is for many a terrible, anxiety-inducing experience into something enjoyable.

The activities can be adapted to any language or level and can be done as supplements to any textbook series or as supplements if you write your own curriculum and materials. Many teachers are throwing away their language textbooks in favor of shifting to proficiency-oriented classes. I would argue that throwing out books and guides is not at all necessary to achieve that end. After all, all of the exercises, vocabulary lists, and supplementary materials are there to lead to real-world proficiency. Textbooks can also serve as a resource, road map, and reference material for students. However, simply completing them does not add up to real-world language skills. Each approach has distinct advantages and disadvantages.

Traditional Textbook v. Teacher-Created and Authentic Resources

Traditional Textbook	Teacher-Created and Authentic Materials
Scope and sequence already done.	Create proficiency-oriented outcomes.
Ancillary materials and ideas included.	Opens door for mainly authentic and comprehensible input.
Getting better all the time.	Adapt, revise, and perfect.
Repertoire of activities to choose from.	Allows for more teacher creativity.
Assessments are included.	Assessments can focus on proficiency-oriented outcomes.
Students and parents love seeing the road map.	Teachers create and curate learning experiences.
Serve as a great resource for learners.	Students and teachers must organize learning materials.
Often mapped out like a race through grammatical structures that students are not ready to master until they reach much higher proficiency levels. Sequence not realistic.	Can be tailored to students' real needs.

Taking a comprehensible input and communicative approach to teaching with a textbook while supplementing with engaging activities and authentic resources is the least stressful way for a language teacher to help students reach intended proficiency targets, in my opinion. As your toolbox grows, so will their language skills.

As you read through the book, you'll find a lot of overlap and ways to use the activities. Don't feel boxed into the categories I have created. Languages don't work that way. While we are teaching listening, reading, speaking, and writing while learning about culture, we are often in several modes simultaneously. For example, we might read about culture, talk about it, and then complete the work with a written assignment. Keep that in mind. You might use a game as an assessment or a speaking activity as a short test. Make these work for you by adapting them to your needs.

Regarding adapting these activities to different levels: Novice/A-level materials deal with words and phrases. Students at this level need a lot of variety in activities and don't have the language to sustain longer activities.

Intermediate/B-level production activities are appropriate for students when they can create with language. Their focus periods in language are longer. Advanced/C-level students can speak in paragraphs. Most of the work in secondary schools is in the first two ranges. Allow more time for more advanced students to produce longer products.

Modes of Communication

ACTFL, the American Council for the Teaching of Foreign Languages, has defined three different modes of communication.

1. Interpersonal. Interactive and dynamic communication between people.
2. Presentational. One person is communicating.
3. Interpretive. What we understand (reading and listening).

While we talk about developing skills in reading, listening, speaking, and writing, thinking about the communicative mode they address provides even more ways to consider their true purpose. As in real life, learners are practicing and performing across different modes of communication. For example, we might watch a film and talk about it (interpretive + interpersonal). We might read a report and write a reaction (interpretive + presentational). While it's important to develop all of these modes and skills, consider trying to integrate skills as often as possible.

Global Themes

The College Board and International Baccalaureate have each identified global themes for language learning.

College Board Global Themes
Personal and Public Identities
Beauty and Aesthetics
Global Challenges
Contemporary Life
Families and Communities
Science and Technology

International Baccalaureate Prescribed Themes
Identities
Experiences
Human Ingenuity
Social Organization
Sharing the Planet

These frameworks provide a structure to design units and lessons for all ranges of proficiency. A unit on the theme of science and technology might have learners acquiring/learning language to talk about weather and seasons for A/Novice learners. A B/Intermediate unit might have learners exploring environmental issues.

Some common themes for A/Novice learners:

- Greetings and Introductions
- Family and Relationships
- Food and Drink
- Daily Routine
- Numbers and Counting
- Colors and Shapes
- Shopping and Clothing
- Transportation
- Weather
- Hobbies and Activities
- Health and Body
- Places and Directions
- Celebrations and Holidays
- Housing and Accommodation
- Personal Descriptions

Some common themes for B/Intermediate learners:

- Daily Life
- Travel and Tourism
- Education and Work
- Current Events and News
- Culture and Customs
- Health and Wellness
- Arts and Entertainment
- Social Issues

Some common themes for C/Advanced learners:

- Literature and Poetry
- Current Affairs and Politics
- History and Culture
- Science and Technology
- Environmental Issues
- Arts and Entertainment
- Social and Psychological Matters

- Business and Economics
- Cross-Cultural Communication
- Advanced Grammar and Linguistics

Cultural Competence

One of the goals of the proficiency-oriented language class is to help learners develop the skills to communicate with speakers of the TL culture. Engaging with authentic resources and people from the TL culture is vital.

Errors

Errors will be referenced throughout this book. I firmly believe that languages are something you must be willing to be bad at first in order to develop any sort of functional skills. Errors are evidence of problem solving, comprehension, effort, and engagement. Empathy + Effort over Extended Time + Engagement + Errors = Excellence. Embracing errors is a pillar of the proficiency-oriented language class.

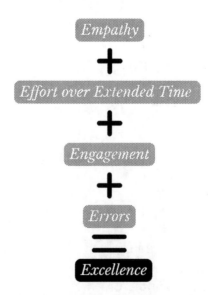

The Es of Language

References

ACTFL. "ACTFL Performance Descriptors for Language Learners." American Council on the Teaching of Foreign Languages, www.actfl.org/educator-resources/actfl-performance-descriptors. Accessed 4 June 2023.

ACTFL. "Reflection—Intercultural Communication." American Council on the Teaching of Foreign Languages, www.actfl.org/uploads/files/general/Resources-Publications/Intercultural-Can-Dos_Reflections-Scenarios.pdf. Accessed 4 June 2023.

AP Central. "AP French Language and Culture." AP French Language and Culture Course, https://apcentral.collegeboard.org/courses/ap-french-language-and-culture?course=ap-french-language-and-culture. Accessed 26 July 2023.

Foreign Service Institute. "Foreign Language Training." U.S. Department of State, www.state.gov/foreign-language-training. Accessed 13 July 2023.

IB Organization. "Language Ab Initio Course." International Baccalaureate®, www.ibo.org/programmes/diploma-programme/curriculum/language-acquisition/language-ab-initio. Accessed 17 July 2023.

IB Organization. "Developing in a Language." International Baccalaureate®, www.ibo.org/programmes/diploma-programme/curriculum/language-acquisition/language-b/#:~:text=The%20language%20B%20syllabus%20is,organization%20and%20sharing%20the%20planet. Accessed 6 December 2023.

Krashen, Stephen. "Stephen Krashen's Theory of Second Language Acquisition." Stephen Krashen, 3 July 2019, www.sk.com.br/sk-krash-english.html. Accessed 16 July 2023.

SECTION 2

The teacher uses the target language as a vehicle of instruction and communication.

2

Lesson Planning and Starting the Year

The beginning of any course or school year can be daunting for both students and teachers. There's often a great deal of expectation. Teachers think: how can I establish a good rapport with students and build communities within classes? They want everyone to progress in their language skills and feel comfortable enough to take risks. They also think about how to ensure that they are understood. They think about Krashen (input) + 1: language and content that is delivered through comprehensible input and therefore easier to understand for students. Language that gives them some problems to solve and at the same time allows the acquisition of more complex language. We also want them to have the linguistic and intercultural skills to access authentic materials and interact with the target language (TL) culture.

Students can also have a great deal of anxiety. If it's a brand-new course or they're new to studying languages, they may have those fears along with excitement and enthusiasm. They may wonder if they will be successful, if their teacher will be kind. They're often scared about making mistakes—a natural part of the process that we need to get comfortable with to be successful in languages. If students took a course in the past, they will likely have had some kind of break between the last course and the new one. There can also be some anxiety about getting back into it. They wonder if they have forgotten everything or if

DOI: 10.4324/9781032622507-4

they need to go back and review all the course materials for last year before starting. These are all normal and natural thoughts we have as language teachers and learners, whether new or returning. Here are some activities to turn this period of time into productive, successful, fun, and low-prep language learning.

Getting Started

When I was a young teacher starting to work in public education, I had an amazing opportunity. My district hired Harry Wong, author of *The First Days of School*. He came to our professional development meeting and talked to us about his ideas, which he says are simple and common sense. And they really are just that—simple and common sense, but so helpful for any teacher. I highly recommend reading his book.

One of my biggest takeaways from his work is his emphasis on routines and procedures. He always states that teachers shouldn't worry about getting right into the content but rather should establish routines, protocols, and procedures in the classroom—for example, how work gets turned in, how we let our teacher know that we need something, how we ask questions, where paper and pencils are, what the materials are like, how they're used, and how we access them. Do we take notes at the beginning of every class? The emphasis should be on ensuring that the people in your class understand the rules and procedures. Once all of that is established, the content will follow.

It may seem like spending two weeks would be a huge loss of time on content. However, this whole concept is the biggest gift in the world for language teachers. We get to teach our target language as we practice all of these procedures. In your target language, lots of classroom commands, relevant language vocabulary and structures are taught and acquired. For example, *push in your chairs, clean off your desk, close your books, open your books*, or *take out paper*. These are all essential survival phrases for any classroom and can be taught in your target language. All of our survival phrases—*Can I get a drink of water? Can I go to the nurse? Can I go to the bathroom?*—can be acquired by learners as well.

Some routines are going through the calendar every day, learning commands and how to do everything in our classroom in the target class language (i.e., bathroom, drink, nurse). Write them specifically into lesson plans every day.

The day I heard Wong speak, he said that students can have enough problems with their friends. Therefore, they don't need any more friends (or the problems that can accompany them), so never ask them how they are. They just need you to let them know that it's nice to see them. This provides language teachers opportunities to teach lots of different positive greetings in the target language. These class routines are also a great opportunity to build a word wall as you go, providing support for learners in the target language.

Regardless of level, establish, practice, and solidify procedures and routines in your classes. Students will acquire and master language through meaningful context and repetition.

Set up Your Classroom

Consider the classroom as a mini TL country, language laboratory, classroom, and theater all in one. When students step into the room, they're going to be learning about new words, new ways of seeing things, new places, geography, and meeting new people. The classroom needs to be conducive to fulfilling these objectives.

Have visual culture. This helps make the room a place where they can see and begin to experience this new culture.

Find posters to adapt and make your own in the digital resources.

The thing that's most essential about the physical environment is that it can be quickly adapted into circles, rows, and tables, and that all of the desks can be pushed out of the way. While we may lecture/give instructions for short periods of time, students need to be able to have dynamic and flexible groupings as well as room for projects, games, and role-plays. It is vital to have ways to change the room easily and quickly. Some configurations to consider:

1. U-shape/horseshoe configuration (round or square) with room for group activities in the center.

2. Small tables made of groups of four desks in a U or circular arrangement that allows for quick transitions to group work, space for activities in the center, and students can still see where you present and display.
3. Deskless classroom with an area to keep something to write on (i.e., lap desks or clipboards).

Have a table where there is everything students could possibly need. Have markers, crayons, colored pencils, a stapler, pencil sharpeners, and a shelf to place extra copies for the entire grading period so students who are absent can easily find them. Have a basket where you place any abandoned pencils or pens. Students without their own can easily get one. This is also the place for things like tissues and tape. Keep recycling paper ready and let students do exercises or take notes on this paper. Students can go there for anything they might require without needing to ask you. These items can also be labeled, providing useful, relevant, comprehensible input.

I am fascinated by languages and always looking for practical ways to create effective experiences for learners to engage with them. Practices that are considered by some to be New Age, such as affirmations, can provide meaningful input. Real-world trends can provide us with so much context to immerse students. Mirrors and doors with positive messages or holiday themes in the target language can teach this vocabulary in context. These can be low-prep when done as a class project and a nice change of pace once routines have been established.

Getting Set up for the Year

Before the year starts, brainstorm and list everything you anticipate needing for your classroom to run smoothly.

This list is by no way exhaustive but can provide a start to the types of things you should take into consideration before the year starts.

◆ How will seating be arranged? Will there be rows? Flexible and dynamic grouping? How often will these groups change? Why and how?

- How will students get things they need (i.e., pencils, paper, forgotten book, computer, etc.)?
- Where will students access key phrases for survival (i.e., getting a drink, going to their locker, going to the nurse, etc.)?
- How will you welcome students to class in the target languages?
- Will your students need to walk in the hall? How will they be trained to do this in the target language?
- How will you take leave with students?
- Will you have a class library in your target language?
- Will TL music be a part of your class routines and atmosphere?
- Do you have a few easy-to-execute differentiation strategies on hand?
- Do you have some templates and activities that can be used for many different activities (i.e., a graphic organizer that can be used for reading, speaking, writing, and listening)?
- How will you deal with early finishers?
- How will you keep students in the target language 90–100% of the time?
- What low-prep/instant activities will you have on hand when there is free time in class?
- How will your room reflect your TL culture(s)?
- How will students access chunks and high-frequency language (i.e., word walls)?
- What will be your class routines? Start of class routines? End of class routines?
- How will students be trained in routines in the target language?
- How will you conduct questioning? What type of wait time will you provide?
- How will students get access to work when they have been absent?
- Where will you display student work?
- How will you redirect behavior when necessary?
- How will you conduct your transitions?

Make your list. Don't worry about perfection, but do try to write down what you will need to consider. You can add to this list each year as your repertoire/toolbox grows.

Review

Teachers don't need to have their knowledge validated by studies in summer learning loss to know that students come back to school needing a fair bit of review. Add to this the loss of time engaged in learning due to the pandemic, and there is much ground to be made up.

This is especially true for language learners after break. Consider listing all of the communicative task objectives from the previous course. For example, going to the doctor's, writing about summer vacation, making travel reservations, and describing relationships might be some of the communicative tasks from the previous course. Treat these tasks as a framework for creating a review unit. Think simulations, student-centered projects, and cultural research activities.

Much of your review will involve combining many components (vocabulary, themes, features and cultural knowledge, and practices) from the previous course. These can make for high-interest activities. Some ideas to perhaps spark yours:

◆ Review vocabulary from two themes and create something fun and original. Perhaps review food, school supplies, body parts, or house vocabulary. Create a person made from one of the other themes or a house made from the other. Make a TL-to-TL key. Up the level by writing about the person or house.
◆ If you have IPAs from the previous course (or can create) to assess each unit, these make for the perfect review activity.
◆ Review units also lend themselves to co-creating with students. List the communicative task to be reviewed. Work with students to decide what acceptable products can be for demonstrating their ability to complete the task, as well as simple criteria for assessment. The grammar,

structures, and vocabulary necessary to complete the task will be a natural context.

A framework based on ACTFL's 5 Cs (*World-Readiness Standards for Learning Languages*) to keep in mind as you plan activities and set up your classroom:

A framework based on ACTFL's 5 C's to keep in mind as you plan activities and set up your classroom:

Communication

This is at the start of the ACTFL standards for a good reason. Everything goes back to being able to communicate with others. Think word walls, cheat sheets, and visual grammar guides. Remember that these can be built as you go through the year based on the needs you identify.

Cultures

Products, practices, and perspectives are essentially what is made, done, and the points of view of its speakers in your target language culture. Have a mix of Big C and Little c. Big C refers to things like history, architecture, and art. Little c is just as important and deals with all we encounter in daily life.

Connections

Languages are so easy to connect to other topics, because students are going to be exploring any theme that you're studying. Your class is also a language arts class, history class, and math class, with a lot of fun, high-interest, current content mixed in.

Comparisons

Students will have many opportunities to explore language and culture. They will become more knowledgeable about English (or another language) from their time in your room.

Communities

Students are learning to use language outside of school, and doing so teaches them further.

A Framework Based on ACTFL's 5 Cs

The ACTFL 5 Cs do a beautiful job of explaining essentials for setting up your room and teaching your courses.

The teacher uses the target language as a vehicle of instruction and communication

ACTFL recommends that language classes, regardless of level, are taught at least 90% in the target language. This can seem daunting. This might seem like an impossibly long day, standing in front of hundreds of students in some cases, speaking your target language. The mere thought of it would exhaust many.

Achieving this 90% does not mean 100% you, sage on the stage, performing all day while trying to make yourself understood. You do not need to speak the entire time to meet this standard. Authentic resources you curate and create and use with the materials you might be required to use can create rich, immersive, and engaging experiences for language learners.

ACTFL defines three modes of communication:

1. Interpretive: what we read and hear.
2. Interpersonal: dynamic back-and-forth communication.
3. Presentational: one person is presenting (writing or speaking).

Consider this as you plan: how can I provide quality input, engaging communicative experiences, and exposure to authentic language and culture via comprehensible input in a way that is sustainable for me and the students? The 10% maximum recommended outside of the target language can be used for directions.

Kindness and Empathy

Kindness and empathy are critical to address in any foreign language class. We have to make a lot of mistakes to be successful in a foreign language. There's no way around it. That polished, fluent speech that we all hope to achieve comes at a cost of exposure and practice over time. To get there, we have to make a lot of errors. It's incredibly important to ensure that there is an atmosphere of kindness and empathy in your class, with you and among your students, so that everyone feels comfortable taking risks. Empathy and learning to see the world through another lens are some of the best takeaways we get from languages, in my opinion.

Lesson Plans

I enjoy working during the summer in and on language learning experiences for myself and other learners. It is the perfect time for me to invest some of my life in creating engaging activities. It allows me to have a life during the school year and not feel behind with creating better systems, routines, and more engaging experiences in languages when my bandwidth is at capacity.

When writing plans, here are my non-negotiables:

1. Plan for units in chunks, starting with the end communicative tasks in mind (McTighe & Wiggin). Assessments and activities should be for building skills to perform those communicative tasks.
2. Consider ACTFL's 5 Cs. Write them in your plans. The purpose is not to create more work for you but to consider what is included in each lesson. They are included there in the lesson plan template for you in the digital resources. Copy, paste, and/or delete for each lesson as appropriate.
3. Consider the modes of communication addressed. Write them (or copy/paste/delete from the template) daily. The purpose is to be thoughtful in how you address each.
4. Establish routines. Write them into your plans. It might feel like they are restrictive at first glance. However, once expectations are established, less time will be spent on transitions. You'll end up with more time to be creative.

Lesson Planning and Starting the Year ◆ 29

5. Leave most explicit grammar lessons for the end of a unit and mini lessons when and where appropriate. The best time to do so is when the students start asking about what the rule is.
6. Repetition is critical. Steve Kaufmann, a linguist studied by Krashen who speaks more than 20 languages, touts its importance. Providing variety to do so is crucial. I suggest planning to revisit and recycle topics over several lessons. Students won't master narrating in the past over a unit. This takes time.

Find the template below. The editable version and some sample lessons for absolute beginners are available for you in the digital resources.

Lesson Plan Template

Course: Subject Name: Date:

ACTFL Standards (change these to your standards if different): Communication, Connections, Culture, Comparisons, Communities
Communicative Objective:

◆ State the specific communicative objective(s) of the lesson.

Modes of Communication Practiced (Presentational, Interpretive, Interpersonal)

Materials:

◆ List the materials, resources, and technology required for the lesson. Link materials anywhere in the lesson where you will use them. This works well for access for absent students as well access in an online classroom. Use year after year, modifying as you go.

1. Routines: Use predictable routines for beginners, such as the calendar and weather. Use more flexible routines for intermediate students.
2. Warm-up Activity: Describe a short activity or discussion to engage students and activate prior knowledge. Is this a video or reading (some type of input)? Is this an interactive chat activity?
3. Introduction:

   - Provide an overview of the lesson and its relevance to students. This is best done as a short, comprehensible input overview of the lesson. I suggest keeping it simple and in bullet points.

4. Presentation:

   - Deliver the content or concept to be taught. This will often be done via input and a communicative task to be fulfilled using that input. Beginners will need more transitions and activities than students who can create with language. This can mean multiple activities to help master the same structures and vocabulary to fulfill a task.

5. Guided Practice:

   - Provide step-by-step instructions and offer support as needed.

6. Independent Practice:

   - Assign activities or tasks that allow students to apply what they have learned.
   - Include a variety of exercises to cater to different learning styles. This can be as simple as product choice. The learners you are with will determine appropriate choices.

Assessment:

◆ Specify how the student's understanding will be assessed. This can be a simple exit ticket, or a small step towards something more comprehensive that you're working to reach.
◆ Outline the criteria or rubric for evaluating student work. Keep it simple. I suggest it be focused on completing communicative tasks and the assessment be focused on feedback. We have to be bad at languages before we are good at them. We have to walk before we can run.

Extension Activities:

◆ Suggest additional activities or resources for students to explore the topic further.

You can display the first page, but this part is just for teachers.

Type in the target language day and date at the top to sneak some input into the lesson.

Consider keeping a running document for each unit/term/quarter/trimester/semester. Essentially, organized by theme, unit, or marking period. Make it easy to manage.

Copy and paste lessons for students when they are absent, or for your online classroom management.

Differentiation:

◆ Describe strategies to support students with diverse needs or learning styles.
◆ Include modifications or extensions for advanced learners or students requiring additional support.

32 ◆ Lesson Planning and Starting the Year

Differentiation

When I first started teaching languages, it occurred to me that I hadn't sufficiently considered that not everyone loved languages as much as I do. Activities that involved reading difficult tasks, having scary conversations, and conjugating verbs intrigued me. I quickly learned that my attitude was not the norm. I needed to adapt my approach fast.

Much of what we do to provide students with the comprehensible input they need to acquire new languages provides multiple entry points for students. Repetition, visuals, real-life scenarios, collaboration, scaffolding, choices, feedback, leverage of technology, and multiple levels of support—commonplace in language learning activities—help learners access language and teachers easily differentiate. The activities throughout this book often have differentiation built in through their design.

Something as simple as allowing students a few choices in what they produce to show their learning can be exactly what a learner needs. For example, allowing a student to tell you about their weekend or write a paragraph about it can be an easy way to differentiate to suit individual preferences. Choosing the type of music they research and share with the class is another. This allows learners to incorporate their own interests and passions into their work. They will produce higher-quality work, as they are more invested.

Beginning language classes can be hard to differentiate with regard to curriculum. We are all individuals and learn things in our own time and in our own way. Inevitably, you will find some students willing and wanting to charge ahead and others working at a different place in their understanding of concepts and themes of the course. As you build a repertoire of activities and get to know students, this will become easier.

Some practical ways to keep all learners engaged and making progress without making you crazy:

1. Flexible and dynamic grouping. Students in the class all work together at some point. It builds community, allowing students to showcase their strengths and learn from each other.

Lesson Planning and Starting the Year ◆ 33

2. Have interesting activities out and ready for fast finishers, such as extra credit crosswords, games, or playlists of music in the target language. Also consider allowing them to do work for other classes at times. Some students will feel as though they are being punished for their hard work if given more work. While this doesn't allow for more time in the target language, giving more work will not result in good outcomes in the long term.
3. Some faster learners will want to move ahead. You likely have materials more advanced than the courses you teach (i.e., reading, grammar books, listening comprehension) for them to further their knowledge. Allowing students to work ahead in your text is another good option.
4. Some students love to be mentors and tutors. Not only does this help them solidify their knowledge, but they can also be great support for their peers.
5. Breaking down tasks into smaller, more manageable steps can help all learners.
6. Provide extra time for completing tasks or assignments if needed.
7. An emphasis on risk-taking, kindness, empathy, and a love of errors will do wonders. Students will feel comfortable asking questions when they need to do so.
8. Some students will need extra tutoring and one-on-one help. Many organizations in schools do this, of course. Teachers also do this. Utilizing native speakers from the community is a great way to build relationships and get these speakers into your class.

Labeling

Whether it is review from a previous course or new, a simple activity like labeling your classroom can be a great way to provide comprehensible input and for students to naturally acquire the language to be used in your class.

A low-prep alternative is to create this with students.

Consider assigning groups in a review class to label as much they can in your classroom and put them up. If you teach

34 ◆ Lesson Planning and Starting the Year

a beginning class, this will help students acquire the language naturally. A more advanced course will have a natural context for review and lots of reminders as they look around your classroom. Have this comprehensible input ready for students.

Redirection/Discipline Procedures

Anytime we might need to redirect students, it's great to have ways to do something in the target language. I know a clever Spanish teacher who quietly gave out yellow and red cards to students as a warning system. It's brilliant because this is a great way to infuse culture (in this case, soccer is extremely popular in the Spanish-speaking world) without it being a disruption. Whatever your procedures are in your school or your class for redirecting students, a great beginning of the year or review activity is to do dramatizations/simulations of these in the target language. For example, you might have two students dramatize a variety of situations that you write down on cards. What's great about it is that it keeps it light but also addresses what may happen in the future while using the target language completely.

Calendar

A great place for using routines and procedures to provide comprehensible input is using your calendar. I learned that the calendar was an indispensable tool for teaching languages from my experience with younger students. Using the calendar daily in your language classes can greatly enhance your program as well. An investment of five minutes or less each day of class time has great returns. A good calendar can teach numbers, patterns, shapes, weather, basic math, days, months, odds or evens. You can incorporate so many things into a short calendar routine every day. Of course, this looks different when students are more proficient, but the point remains the same. Invest a little bit of time in talking about the calendar every day in your target language, and you'll find that you can almost skip over these bits in your textbook or spend a very short amount of time and do some engaging projects instead. You can

Lesson Planning and Starting the Year ◆ 35

then assign fun, immersive projects and activities later in the year as well (i.e., weather reports, projects on seasons, write about what you do on different days of the week, etc.). These projects also make for wonderful sub plans. The students will produce great products since they already know the vocabulary needed well. Students also receive an introduction to the past and future tenses with this calendar work. By investing a couple of minutes every day, students will learn all of this language in context.

Focus on a different section each day of the calendar as you start, and add an activity or two to help with the vocabulary. This is a great place for a song, dance, rhyme, or choral repetition—whatever you do to help students remember vocabulary.

You can start with a simple calendar done with a word-processing program. Some options are to print it out (small or poster size) and draw (or have students do so) weather icons, etc. We have provided you with some editable templates in the digital resources.

Using the calendar with more advanced students might be selecting a time period about which to chat. For example, chats about holidays provide relevant communicative practice as well as potential for comparing and contrasting cultural norms. Use the calendar to inspire chats to develop knowledge about cultures as well as grammar points, time frames, and tenses.

GENNAIO

LUNEDI	MARTEDI	MERCOLEDI	GIOVEDI	VENERDI	SABATO	DOMENICA
31	1	2	3	4	5	6
7	8	9	10	11	12	13
14	15	16	17	18	19	20
21	22	23	24	25	26	27
28	29	30	1	2	3	4

Calendar

36 ◆ Lesson Planning and Starting the Year

More Routines

The calendar is mostly geared toward Novice/A learners. Routines in an Intermediate/B-level course will look quite different. This will be something that is low-prep, engaging, and allows students practice in at least one mode of communication.
Some examples:

1. **Free Voluntary Reading/Reading Cart/Class Library.** Allowing students to engage in input is a popular routine. Some teachers invest in class libraries with comprehensible novels or authentic content such as magazines and cookbooks. A low-prep option is using online resources, such as news sites online in different languages. Your prep might be finding appropriate TL keywords to help students find reading relevant to your theme.
2. **Journal writing.** Naturally, journals look quite different in the world language classroom than in other contexts since learners need support with language. Novice learners will need a lot of support. Essentially, journaling might be completing a quick task in the target language. We will explore some ways to do this in Chapter 8 on Grammar, Listening, and Writing. Many second-language students need some quiet time to process before speaking, so this type of routine can be vital on the road to fluency.
3. **Conversation Cards.** This is one of those activities that you invest in once and can keep for years. Brainstorm questions on your themes. Use a voice-to-text app to get them from your brain onto paper. You'll likely need to edit them before sharing with students.

   - Option #1. Copy and paste onto slides. You will now have a set of quick warmups to do as a whole class. You can also print these out (six slides per page) or print on cardstock and laminate. Drop some of these cards in the middle of tables for students to chat about in groups.
   - Option #2. Print out sheets of questions for students. They can quietly answer the questions as journal prompts.

4. **Chat Slides.** Simple slides of common themes are a great way to get them talking. Find a picture and add some questions to speech bubbles. Pictures provide great prompts for speaking.

   Some alternatives are *Would you rather…?/This or that?* slides: use a simple slide template with a text box and space for two photos. You can even use simple lists to begin. Use the same slide template for questions where students can be provided with choices to discuss things they might want, prefer, or will do in the future.

   Creating slide presentations, while becoming easier all the time due to apps and technology becoming more and more intuitive, is time-consuming. Either invest in creating chat slides once, knowing you'll use them for years, or have them made for you. I highly recommend creating a template and listing your questions/prompts. Go to a freelance site and have them made for you. Templates for further ideas are included in the digital resources.

5. **Listening Task.** I love being a linguist in today's world. It has never been easier to access authentic language and culture, all with a simple Internet connection. The tools to make this input comprehensible are becoming more and more effective and accurate all the time. Think about how easy it is to make speech slower or add captions. You can pause and repeat as much as you need to understand, acquiring more and more language each time.

   Your materials may have an online "lab" built in, making this an easy no-/low-prep routine to implement. If not, consider a generic listening graphic organizer (included in the Templates section) or do a short listening activity with students (more shared in Chapter 8 on Grammar, Listening, and Writing).

Co-creating Courses, Lessons, Units, and Projects

Many courses come with required textbooks. As we move into the upper-intermediate/B1 to B2 and Advanced/C-range, there is often much freedom and flexibility in the theme and content used to build proficiency at these higher levels.

A project that caught my attention was the creation of two upper-level university-level Spanish courses. One was focused on raciolinguistics (Dr. Stephanie Knouse, Furman University) and the other on achieving Advanced-Low (ACTFL) oral proficiency in Spanish through a course on social justice (Dr. Begoña Caballero-García, Wofford College). While many teachers will not have the license or freedom to design such courses, there are some excellent takeaways for teachers at all levels:

1. These professors both designed their course after having done Action Research, identifying the needs of their own students.
2. The professors included their non-negotiables. Students had freedom to help create the content of the course after having been presented with a strong framework. Voice and choice foster interest.
3. Once the outcomes were established, grading criteria were co-created, with professor non-negotiables and student input. This step allows for a lot of detailed communication about the outcomes, helping students have a deep investment and understanding of what they will produce.
4. Dr. Caballero-García introduced herself at the beginning of her course via email. What an excellent opportunity for input in context!
5. All modes of communication were developed in the courses through speaking, reading, listening, and writing, all in context.
6. The professors initially started small with teaching languages through the lens of social justice.
7. Both professors and their students reflected regularly to provide the most effective and impactful experiences for learners.

These takeaways can be used to create smaller units and lessons on any topic in your course not at such a high level of inquiry as social justice in a target language. It might start as simple as a couple of classes in which students select a specific task they want to be able to do in the target language, providing them with a structure and framework within to work and co-create the criteria for assessing the outcome.

If you are interested in learning further about social justice in the language classroom, Dr. Knouse has curated a rich set of resources to get started. Please see the link in the digital resources.

A few closing thoughts:

1. Invest in routines and low- and no-prep games to maximize time in the target language.
2. My best ideas come from being a learner of languages myself. Nothing will generate more ideas than experiencing languages through that lens. Connections to real-world experiences are the fastest route to proficiency.
3. Some activities that seem like fluff and filler actually lower affect, making language easier to acquire. Engaging students in communicating in the target language builds proficiency.

References

ACTFL. "World-Readiness Standards for Learning Languages." American Council on the Teaching of Foreign Languages, www.actfl.org/educator-resources/world-readiness-standards-for-learning-languages.

Knouse, Stephanie M. "Achieving the W-RSLLs through Social Justice Education." Google Docs, docs.google.com/document/d/1nmOQ2CjkoRoofg6s8O-0n0ktNeGNQRAP681JarRPJpY/edit. Accessed 28 July 2023.

Krashen, Stephen. "Stephen Krashen's Theory of Second Language Acquisition." Stephen Krashen, 3 July 2019, www.sk.com.br/sk-krash-english.html. Accessed 16 July 2023.

Wong, Harry K. *The First Days of School:* Harry K Wong Publications, 2018.

Wiggins, Grant P., and Jay McTighe. *Understanding by Design.* Association for Supervision and Curriculum Development, 2008.

SECTION 3

Members feel comfortable risk-taking in the target language.

DOI: 10.4324/9781032622507-5

3

Low- and No-Prep Games

While it takes strong and developed language skills to teach languages at the advanced level, the real work is in getting learners started. We're so often dealing with fears and getting through feelings of failure for trying to communicate as well as people do in their native language(s). There is also the simple fact that while we're in the Novice/A range, we begin with nothing and end the level with a bank of words and phrases in our target language with which learners can begin to create their own messages.

Language classes in primary and secondary education are often geared toward this skill range. Since Intermediate/B learners can create sentences and build up to paragraphs and Advanced/C are working in paragraphs, their activities should reflect that. These learners can spend more time working independently and productively. Novice/A learners need a great deal of support. They need a variety of activities to keep them engaged and immersed in language appropriate for their skill level.

The bottom line: teachers working with these beginners need a repertoire of activities that require little to no prep and can be done anytime there is time to spare or life needs to be infused into practice. The content can be that last vocabulary page often found at the end of chapters in textbooks.

To differentiate for different proficiency ranges, consider the input and output students will have. The input should provide some opportunities for problem solving, and the final output product will be commensurate. Intermediate/B range students

DOI: 10.4324/9781032622507-6

will be working in sentences up to paragraphs. Advanced students will be working in paragraphs to connected paragraphs.

The games and activities listed here require little or no prep and can be adapted to any language. Many of these won't be new. However, I am going to ask you to develop a stronger relationship with them, as they can serve as a lifeline in your classes. They keep students in the target language and lower affect.

No-Prep Games

There is often a textbook or communicative themes that provide a roadmap for a course. Many teachers who are working within a framework have specific vocabulary that might be summarized in a list for each chapter or section.

This list is a goldmine of no-prep instant games that engage learners. Pick at least ten to learn and always have on hand for when you need them. It might be a five- or ten-minute period of class that would otherwise be less productive. Those short time periods add up toward meeting your proficiency goals.

Charades

This basically involves one person or group of people acting out a vocabulary word or a situation and others guessing what it is in the target language. Cut up slips of recycled paper and hand them to teams to act out and guess, or use a list of your common words to play.

Pictionary Three Ways

#1: Someone illustrates a word and someone else guesses it. This works in small or large groups.

#2: Pair Pictionary can be played with your target vocabulary for your unit.

Give students a printout of the chapter vocabulary (ideal) or use a vocabulary page from text.

Divide into teams of two, with one player on each team acting as the artist and the other as the guesser. If there is an odd number of students, one can be the scorekeeper and check off the words that have already been guessed.

Give them rounds of one or two minutes. The artist on the chosen team will then pick a word or phrase within that category and draw it on the whiteboard or paper.

The team with the most points at the end of the game wins.

#3: Backward/Reverse Pictionary is a variation of Pictionary that serves as great listening comprehension that you can do as the leader. They draw what you say. You can also have your students do it in small groups or pairs. If you have small whiteboards, great (but beware of a lot of markers being used at once). Paper, or anything else you can draw on, works well, too.

Instant Games: Post-its and Index Cards

For all of these games, consider using index cards (they will last to be reused for years). Keep them in small bags.

#1: When you have a few minutes and have to review, have students write out questions based on the content you're doing. They then place their Post-its/index cards on the board. Divide up the teams based on the geography of your class.

Give each team a specific number of turns (i.e., 2, 3, etc.). You ask the team questions, granting a point for each correct. Once their turns are up, go to another team.

#2: After ensuring that the review objectives are understood and students have access to their materials, pass out Post-it notes or index cards. The number will depend on the size of your class.

Next, create six categories based on your review materials.

Students will write answers to questions found in the materials on Post-its (great for no prep) or index cards (keep for years).

Place these in rows and columns, like the classic Jeopardy game. You may need to do some on-the-spot editing of the material. Place values in ascending order to the questions.

Divide the class into teams. Students earn points by asking the correct questions.

This activity can be easily adapted to any topic, theme, grammar point, language, and proficiency range.

Category 1	Category 2	Category 3	Category 4	Category 5	Category 6
1. Answer 1	1. Answer 1	1. Answer 1	1. Answer 1	1. Answer 1	1. Answer 1
2. Answer 2	2. Answer 2	2. Answer 2	2. Answer 2	2. Answer 2	2. Answer 2
3. Answer 3	3. Answer 3	3. Answer 3	3. Answer 3	3. Answer 3	3. Answer 3
4. Answer 4	4. Answer 4	4. Answer 4	4. Answer 4	4. Answer 4	4. Answer 4
5. Answer 5	5. Answer 5	5. Answer 5	5. Answer 5	5. Answer 5	5. Answer 5

Final Jeopardy

Final Jeopardy Category
Final Jeopardy Answer _____

Jeopardy Game Template

Use this template as a framework. Enlarge with your answers and add Post-it notes with dollar amounts to cover each box. Remove Post-its to reveal prompts. Students earn points for providing the correct question to the answer. I recommend being flexible with how you play, as Novice/A students are still learning to create with language.

#3: If you teach an intermediate/advanced class, you will surely teach tactful problem resolution and giving advice at some point.

Have students write problems on Post-it notes/index cards. Invented problems (i.e. the paparazzi won't stop following me) with some hyperbole are often high-interest. Simple works well, too.

Students then have to place their Post-it notes/index cards in a specific area. Every student then takes someone else's problem

46 ◆ Low- and No-Prep Games

and goes back to their seat. They read through the problem and formulate a response. Sit in a circle and share the problem and the solutions or practice letter writing to provide advice. This language lesson provides practice for many skills and helps them develop extended discourse necessary in the Advanced/C range.

Some ideas for contexts within common themes:

- ◆ Being a successful student.
- ◆ Staying healthy.
- ◆ Doing housework.
- ◆ How to protect our environment.
- ◆ Choosing a college major or career.
- ◆ Playing a sport or another activity.
- ◆ Making new friends.
- ◆ Helping two friends make up after a disagreement.
- ◆ Your exchange student roommate feels shy about speaking. What would you recommend?
- ◆ How to read in a new language.
- ◆ How to train a dog to behave.

Another low-prep alternative is to create a collaborative presentation in which students write their prompts, questions, and/or answers on slides. Do a quick edit and print out six slides per page for card size. Laminate, cut, and add to your repertoire.

Scattergories/Categories

Beginners will need a lot more support than more advanced learners (as in all the activities), but you can still play this with almost absolute beginners if they've got access to a textbook or other tool to find vocabulary. Focus your categories on specific parts of your text or materials and allow them some time to reference these tools.

Give the letter, theme, and a time. Groups brainstorm to find as many things as they can that go into that category. For beginners, an example might be vegetables. Within that time, the group will write down as many vegetables as they can in the target language. You can also have a goal of at least one per category. Award points for unique answers.

Category:

1. A_____
2. B_____
3. C_____
4. D_____
5. E_____
6. F_____
7. G_____
8. H_____
9. I_____
10. J_____
11. K_____
12. L_____
13. M_____
14. N_____
15. O_____
16. P_____
17. Q_____
18. R_____
19. S_____
20. T_____
21. U_____
22. V_____
23. W_____
24. X_____
25. Y_____
26. Z_____

Adapt the template to suit your language/alphabet.

See three different Scattergories templates (letters, beginning letters, communicative themes) in the digital resources.

CharPictionary/Taboo

#1: My understanding of this game is that it's basically Charades and Pictionary with the use of props. Students can use drawings, visuals, props, or actions to convey the meaning of their chosen word. To make it low prep, use the vocabulary page from your textbook (many are now digital). Check off as words are guessed or cut into small strips and used to count points as you play. Choose your taboo words and include them, or don't—just have them work with your vocabulary list.

#2: A variation on this is to have students prepare definitions in their target language beforehand. This is a fun, no-prep activity to practice circumlocution—a critical skill for building advanced-level proficiency in any language.

#3: Using that same pre-generated list of words in card/strip form, split the class into teams, and get a timer.

The cards consist of a word or phrase that players must get their team to guess, along with a list of "taboo" words that cannot be used as clues. Divide players into two teams and choose a timekeeper. Each team will take turns being the guessing team and the clue-giving team.

Decide on the game's duration or number of rounds. Typically, a game consists of multiple rounds, and each round has a time limit (one or two minutes).

◆ The clue-giving team selects a player to start. This player draws a word or phrase from the deck and tries to get their team to guess the main word without using any of the taboo words listed.

Low- and No-Prep Games ◆ 49

- The clue-giver begins giving clues to their team. They can use verbal descriptions, actions, or gestures to convey the meaning of the word without directly saying it or any of the taboo words.
- The clue-giver's team members try to guess the word correctly within the given time limit. They earn points for correct answers. They can also pass and move on to the next card, but won't receive any points for that word.
- The opposing team and teachers ensure that the clue-giver does not say any of the taboo words. If the clue-giver makes a mistake and says one, the opposing team can point it out. The clue-giver must then draw a new word and continue.

Continue playing until all the words have been used or until time runs out. Adapt the rules (i.e. gestures v. no gestures, length of rounds, etc.) to suit your class.

Bingo

We all know Bingo is a fun way to get in a much-needed change of pace while learning vocabulary at the Novice-level. Here are a few reasons to include it regularly in your beginning-level classes:

1. Instant Total Physical Response
TPR is a beginning language teacher's best friend. Total Physical Response involves the learner having to respond to something in the target language, of course. A lot of computer programs (e.g., Rosetta Stone) use this method.

Bingo works for any theme and can easily be adapted to supplement any curriculum or textbook.

At the most basic level, Bingo is TPR. Students hear and see words and take action based on the prompt. They are attentive; they are listening and engaged in the target language.

You can teach many concepts using Bingo, and visuals make it great comprehensible input. You can teach grammar and verb tenses using Bingo as well. It is a useful tool to create effective, engaging lessons for beginners.

2. Make the difficult parts less so

Some difficult concepts that can be taught through Bingo and shave days off attainment of student mastery are the alphabet in foreign languages, time, verb tenses, and adjectives, just to name a few.

3. Bingo can be communicative and interactive

Make a simple grid on paper (3 x 3, 4 x 4, etc.), or make one in a word-processing program using tables. Students can fill it in with whatever you're working on. You can co-create this with students by deciding what the bank of content will be.

Low- and No-Prep Games ◆ 51

Bingo Grid

52 ◆ Low- and No-Prep Games

It's great to pull out Bingo when you've got a few extra minutes in class. It keeps everyone engaged and learning. Give fun prizes like pencils and erasers and bookmarks with the target language on them.

Bingo is fun. You won't feel like you're lecturing. Students won't feel like you're lecturing, and everyone will be learning and having a good time at the same time.

Races

Races give everyone a chance to be up and moving around and can be adapted to any world language lesson. Races can be translations, verb conjugations, TL script, or vocabulary. They can be interpretive or presentational.

#1: *Flyswatter* or *Touch a Word* are common ways to use TPR/ Races for Novice learners. You can use items from your classroom, a transparency, or drawings made by students that represent the target vocabulary. Put them on the ground. The students swat/ touch the words you say.

#2: Display things on a digital whiteboard and have learners identify them. They get in two lines and the teacher says a word in the target language. They have to come up and be the first one to touch it. Many textbooks have some digital vocabulary resources.

#3: An easy, no-prep game is to split the class into teams. Students decide the order in which they will answer questions. They run to the board and respond. Teams get points for correct answers first. Consider allowing them to study (i.e., their vocabulary page) when they are in certain positions in the line.

Two (or Three) Truths and a Lie

#1: Students write out two (or three) truths and a lie and they share, then decide as a class if it is true or not and why? Guess which one is the lie.

#2: Play a different variation of this for a low Novice level that I call *Is it True?*

Low- and No-Prep Games ◆ 53

Whatever vocabulary you're teaching, make a list of statements, some true and some false, that they can easily understand using your target vocabulary theme and grammar—for example, *this person likes hamburgers*, *this person likes tacos*. They have to think about the people they know in their class and decide if it's true or not. An example is included in the activity "Is it True?" in Chapter 8.

#3: To make this activity for students beyond the Novice range, divide the students into different groups. The students are going to do a more extended version of their *Two (or Three) Truths and a Lie*.

This works well when students are learning to narrate in the past. Provide them with a task (e.g., a good day, bad day, trip) and some guiding questions to help them structure their responses to begin. Divide students into groups of three or four.

For example, if you had two groups, in one group, one student would have the lie and two of them would have true stories. In the other group, two (or three) students would lie and one would have a true story. Students will adapt their stories to contain an identifiable lie (I suggest coaching the students to ensure the lie will be obvious). Of course, the objective is to guess the lie. There's a great deal of listening, speaking, and collaborating that goes on to figure out which stories are true and which are lies.

Buzzers, Bells, Balls, and Other Fun Things

It is essential to have a few fun gadgets on hand to gamify dry textbook activities and sets of questions and answers, vocabulary recall, etc. A Hot Potato, Koosh ball, hotel-style bell, or buzzer can serve as the perfect lift when you need to infuse some energy into class.

Use this for any vocab recall you have. When the music goes off (someone catches a ball or however you want to determine turns), the students start asking questions, making for a naturally communicative activity for the world language class. Use pictures (they can keep the pictures to count points).

When you get the Hot Potato (or when it is your turn), you might say three things about yourself, or some other task.

Students might ask the person with the potato a certain number of questions. A Koosh ball can be easily passed around without risk of injury.

I love looking at corporate training and what little I do know about working for companies for this. Making learning more interactive in the form of games, team points, and tangible rewards increases engagement for learners of all ages.

There are some cute and clever apps out there. I love all of the online timers, countdown apps, and spinners. They can help you easily time rounds of games or call on teams.

Don't have access to a spinner? Draw a quick one on the board.

Consider getting a sticky ball. It is exactly what it sounds like. It sticks to the whiteboard when thrown. They can make fun, instant TPR activities and games.

On the YouTube channel ESL Guys with Games, they combined these concepts in a clever way. Draw a large pie, and write student names or vocabulary words in the slices. Where the sticky ball lands determines the question or who responds.

Low-Prep Games/Activities

The following activities require a bit of prep. In some cases, more than a little. However, these activities can be used over and over for years, so they're worth the investment.

Flashcards and Card Games

#1: While flashcards are traditional and old school, I believe that there is value in creating them. Not only do they help students acquire some language through input, but they also provide opportunities for traditional language learning. Students can quiz each other in pairs, do ping-pong activities, and play engaging games with their creations.

Use any type of card, but index cards are often best. Make cards with different languages on each side. Using those same cards, play a game like Flyswatter or Touch a Word.

#2: Another way to use language flash cards as a teacher is to have just the picture or just the picture on one and the word on another one. After students have made the cards, they can play Concentration/Memory (they turn them over and match pairs).

#3: After making the cards, divide your class into two teams. A student from each team comes to the front. With cards behind their backs, they turn around at your signal. The first student to say the word on the other's card (or both) wins. They keep both cards to count points.

Card games are fabulous for language learners. They provide a purpose, context, interaction, reading, listening, and speaking. At the most basic level, these games can be played with simple pairs of flashcards:

#4: Those same cards that you used for Concentration/ Memory can be used to play Go Fish. Shuffle them up. Everyone starts with seven. Put the extra ones in the middle. Say in the target language the equivalent of *Do you have…?* or *Do you see…? (Do you want…?* etc.). *Yes, I have… I don't have… Yes, I see…* or *I don't see…* etc. If you don't, go fish.

Some formats to consider:

◆ Basic questions and answers (matching).
◆ Pairs (Do you want/see/have…?).
◆ Pairs (How do you say…? in the target language).
◆ Pictures and words.

Some hacks to consider to lower prep time for these:

◆ Have students make them. If each student does two pairs (use index cards), you have a set you can use for years. They'll also benefit from creating them.
◆ Consider sites like Fiverr, or another where you can outsource tasks. You can simply provide a list to someone of the presentation you want made from royalty-free photos. You then have a presentation. You can print this presentation (six slides each) on card stock, laminate, and cut. Your sets will last for years and be well worth the investment.

#5: *Les Sept Familles* (The Seven Families) is a French card game.

The game is played with a deck of 42 cards that are divided into seven different families. You can use any category you wish to create a "family." It can be an actual family, verb conjugations, emotions, professions, or any other vocabulary you choose.

Shuffle the deck of cards and deal them out to all players evenly. Each player should have the same number of cards in their hand. There should be enough left for a pile of cards to draw from.

The object of the game is to collect all seven cards of any one family. The first player to do so is the winner.

The game begins with the player to the left of the dealer. This player asks any other player for a specific card that they need to complete a set.

If the player being asked has the requested card, they must give it to the player who asked for it. If not, the player who asked must draw a card from the deck.

If the player who asked for the card receives it, they get another turn to ask for a card. This continues until the player either cannot ask for another card or they complete a set of seven cards. Once a player has collected all seven cards of a family, they lay them on the table face-up and declare that they have completed the family. They are then the winner.

Adapt the rules to suit your players. There are often variations of the rules for all of these games. I suggest allowing for a bit of student negotiation. The point, after all, is for them to be engaged in learning to communicate in the target language.

Tasks

Tasks are, in my opinion, the single most powerful way to build skills in a language. An authentic task is meant to fulfill a real, communicative need. One of the most successful language programs that I am aware of is from the Church of Latter-Day Saints. They work with tasks to build real-world language proficiency to go out on their missions, spreading the word of their religion to people all over the world. They must connect, engage, and persuade. The takeaways for language learners are powerful. Authentic communicative tasks build skills.

Low- and No-Prep Games ◆ 57

ACTFL describes the tasks that we do in our classrooms as *performance tasks*.

Here is a list of micro-tasks for beginners to get you started:

Below are the things that we will learn to say in this class:

- ❑ Name the countries that speak the target language.
- ❑ Name the capitals of the countries that speak the target language.
- ❑ Greet people in the morning.
- ❑ Greet someone in the afternoon.
- ❑ Greet someone in the evening.
- ❑ Ask someone what their name is.
- ❑ Say what your name is.
- ❑ Say the word for *you* formal.
- ❑ Say the word for *you* informal.
- ❑ Ask someone how they are (formal).
- ❑ Ask someone how they are (informal).
- ❑ Say how you are.
- ❑ Take leave.
- ❑ Tell someone that you are pleased to meet them.
- ❑ Have a conversation in which you meet someone for the first time.
- ❑ Say basic classroom commands.
- ❑ Count to ten.
- ❑ Count to 20.
- ❑ Say your phone number.
- ❑ Say at least five body parts.
- ❑ Say the names for at least five things you use at school.
- ❑ Ask how something is said in the target language.
- ❑ Say the alphabet in the target language.
- ❑ Spell your name in the target language.
- ❑ Spell the names of your family members in the target language.
- ❑ Say the days of the week.
- ❑ Say the months of the year.
- ❑ Ask what day it is.

58 ◆ Low- and No-Prep Games

- ❏ Ask what the date is.
- ❏ Say today and tomorrow.
- ❏ Ask what the weather is like.
- ❏ Say what the weather is like.
- ❏ Say the seasons.
- ❏ Say the verbs for basic activities.
- ❏ Say what you like to do.
- ❏ Ask someone what they like to do.
- ❏ Introduce yourself.
- ❏ Say what foods you don't like.
- ❏ Agree.
- ❏ Disagree.
- ❏ Describe your personality.
- ❏ Say *the* in the target language.
- ❏ Say the names of your classes.
- ❏ Describe your classes.
- ❏ Say I.
- ❏ Say the names for at least ten items in your classroom.
- ❏ Say *a* and *an* in the target language.
- ❏ Say what five possessions you have are.
- ❏ Ask what.
- ❏ Ask who.
- ❏ Ask which.
- ❏ Ask when.
- ❏ Ask what something is.
- ❏ Ask what there is or there are.
- ❏ Ask how many.
- ❏ Ask where/where is…
- ❏ Ask why…
- ❏ Say two things you love.
- ❏ List five foods.
- ❏ Say the names of two meals.
- ❏ Say the names of four drinks.
- ❏ Say three things that other people do at school using the present tense.
- ❏ Say two basic physical exercises.

Low- and No-Prep Games ◆ 59

- ❏ Tell us that you are hungry.
- ❏ Tell us that you are thirsty.
- ❏ Tell us that you are tired.
- ❏ Tell us the time.
- ❏ What do you eat in the morning?
- ❏ What do you eat in the afternoon?
- ❏ What do you eat in the evening?
- ❏ Express your opinions on food.
- ❏ State the things that you have in your locker.
- ❏ State the things that other people do in their homes.
- ❏ Where do your friends go?
- ❏ Say when you do activities during the day (i.e., your routine).
- ❏ Say the names of two sports you like.
- ❏ Express to someone that you are sorry.
- ❏ Describe how you are feeling.

Printing out these mini-tasks and cutting them up (or writing them on cards) can serve as a quick assessment, warm-up, or game.

The Can-Do Game

I love the Can-Do statements. If you're unfamiliar with them, ACTFL/NCSSFL has published an extensive list.

Essentially, they illustrate many different tasks that people can do as they're moving in the stages toward fluency in a language. It's absolutely amazing. You need to judge the level your students are at, of course, before playing this.

Write these tasks down on pieces of paper (or cut them up from the printed document). Fold the papers up and have learners prep and/or perform those tasks. Co-create criteria for mastery.

You might want to start with letting them read through and practice before playing the game. Consider co-creating a points system with students based on thoroughness.

Tic-Tac-Toe Four Ways

If you are unfamiliar with Dr. Rassias, he was an amazing leader in teaching foreign languages. He made learning active and immersive. His activities with comprehensible input (a sort of early TPRS with lots of visuals) get people speaking fast and accurately. While Dr. Rassias did not invent the game, he had a great take on it.

#1: Put students in pairs. They identify vocabulary or verbs. Give them a list. They get X's and O's. The winner is obviously just like traditional tic-tac-toe. Do several rounds for repetition.

You can also do your tic-tac-toe with complex structure translations. They get it right, they get to place the X or the O. Infuse culture here by making X's and O's cultural (i.e., clip art, baguettes, flags, or shapes in the target language).

#2: Have students work in teams against teams. As you're busy, you can also allow one student to be the moderator. That person has a bank of words, questions, or tasks in hand and can serve as the judge. It's a sneaky way to get more study in.

#3: Create reusable boards out of laminated card stock and poster board representing target culture flags, but paper or white boards work well also. Divide students into small groups. Four is ideal for small groups, but you can divide the class into two teams and play as a group. Each team gets an X or O, or the equivalent of such. Use items in the class to help review vocabulary and/or grammar.

The students (or you) should ask each other the TL word. They can use any of the methods mentioned above (i.e., draw, act out, etc.) but I suggest something simple like *How do you say...?* When a team gets a correct answer, they can put down their X or O. For teaching, make a board with squares that look like TL country flags.

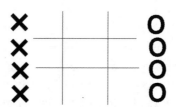

Beat the Teacher

Low- and No-Prep Games ◆ 61

#4: Beat the Teacher: This variation of Tic Tac Toe is a fun game from a British television show for school children.

Take your content set. It can be materials from your text, or something you want them to master. For this example, we'll use the imperfect tense in Spanish. You'll start with the answer sheet (only you'll have this).

Hand out the student response sheet. Make a Tic-Tac-Toe board (or use mine). They get an answer, they put down an X or O. You're right, you put yours down. They should write the answers in the blanks. Keep a blank answer sheet ready to reuse each time you play (I like 30 spaces). Keep playing for mastery.

Imperfect Verbs Answer Sheet

1. hablaba—I used to speak
2. hablabas—You used to speak
3. hablaba—He/She/You (formal) used to speak
4. hablábamos—We used to speak
5. hablaban—They/You all (formal) used to speak
6. comía—I used to eat
7. comías—You used to eat
8. comía—He/She/You (formal) used to eat
9. comíamos—We used to eat
10. comían—They/You all (formal) used to eat
11. escribía—I used to write
12. escribías—You used to write
13. escribía—He/She/You (formal) used to write
14. escribíamos—We used to write
15. escribían—They/You all (formal) used to write
16. iba—I used to go
17. ibas—You used to go
18. iba—He/She/You (formal) used to go
19. íbamos—We used to go

62 ◆ Low- and No-Prep Games

20. iban—They/You all (formal) used to go
21. era—I used to be
22. eras—You used to be
23. era—He/She/You (formal) used to be
24. éramos—We used to be
25. eran—They/You all (formal) used to be
26. veía—I used to see
27. veías—You used to see
28. veía—He/She/You (formal) used to see
29. veíamos—We used to see
30. veían—They/You all (formal) used to see

Beat the Teacher Student Answer Sheet

1. _____	16. _____
2. _____	17. _____
3. _____	18. _____
4. _____	19. _____
5. _____	20. _____
6. _____	21. _____
7. _____	22. _____
8. _____	23. _____
9. _____	24. _____
10. _____	25. _____
11. _____	26. _____
12. _____	27. _____
13. _____	28. _____
14. _____	29. _____
15. _____	30. _____

Hangman

This is a must-do classic. Work it into your repertoire if you don't already do it. If you and the students have writing tools and a list of words to reference (i.e., your vocabulary page), that's all you need.

EL AHORCADO

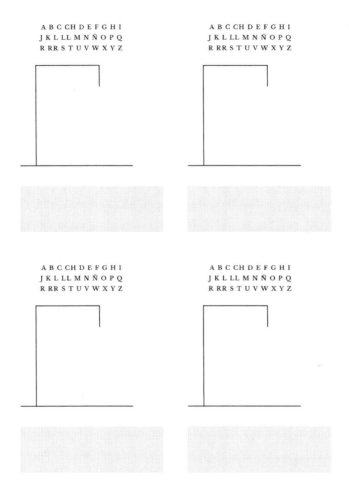

Hangman

Hangman can get a makeover in a couple of ways. You might spell the words for the students to guess, making it a listening activity.

Hangman can also have a more politically correct makeover by building something cute in lieu of the hangman.

References

ACTFL. *Reflection: Intercultural Communication*. American Council on the Teaching of Foreign Languages, www.actfl.org/uploads/files/general/Resources-Publications/Intercultural-Can-Dos_Reflections-Scenarios.pdf. Accessed 4 June 2023

ACTFL. *ACTFL Performance Descriptors for Language Learners*, American Council on the Teaching of Foreign Languages, www.actfl.org/uploads/files/general/ACTFLPerformance_Descriptors.pdf. Accessed 4 June 2023.

Guys with Games ESL. "ESL Games (GWG) #67 Stickyball Pizza." YouTube, 25 October 2020, www.youtube.com/watch?v=iPKUbE7Hsk4. Accessed 4 June 2023.

SECTION 4

Communication is the main focus of class.

DOI: 10.4324/9781032622507-7

4

Student-Centered Communicative Activities

Bringing students into deep language learning/acquisition means a lot of engagement from them. While some will come to our classes naturally seeking that, it is not always easy to maintain for Novice/A-range learners. Other students will come to our classes without having the desire to really learn at all. These activities can provide rich, deep learning activities that can be adapted to any language and can be used in a classroom or in any remote or hybrid learning space.

Feelings/Emotions

#1: The student makes a Google slide presentation showing people asking and answering how they are. The student narrates their slides. The student speaks no English in the video.

#2: Create a Google slide and invite the entire class to collaborate.

Each student will create one slide. The slide must show an emotion and be correctly captioned in the target language. Once all the slides are done, make corrections. Narrate the slides and export as a video.

Share this collaborative CI (comprehensible input) presentation teaching emotions with the class.

DOI: 10.4324/9781032622507-8

#3: Students make drawings (fun for our talented artists) or take photos of emotions (theirs or others'). Caption in the target language.

#4: My(selfie). Students can take or use a selfie to start. They must also select three images that represent them on the inside. They must then present these photos and describe why they selected these photos in the target language.

Allow them to do their presentations from their phones. They can also create a presentation.

Students can also do their own drawings—a good option for our artists.

Spanish with Stephanie does a fun activity with this to teach grammar. Students take selfies. Add pictures to slides. Students write their emotions and self-descriptions in a speech bubble, deciding which Spanish verb expressing "to be" is necessary.

Family

Basic family trees are fun and worthwhile. Below are a few variations on this classic.

#1: My Family

The student creates a book, oral presentation, slide show, video, or report (oral or written) featuring at least two members of their family.

Book: The student includes a drawing of each person. The student tells the names of each family member and writes at least five sentences to describe each person. The student tells where each person is from and includes at least one of their likes.

Presentation/slide show: The student creates a slide to represent each person in their family. The slide is narrated based on the topics above.

Be specific with the tasks to include. This is a great opportunity to recycle vocabulary, grammar, and relevant language chunks you want them to acquire. Some things to consider include: feelings, where people live, professions, hobbies, accomplishments, daily routines, special talents, pets, travels, or skills.

68 ◆ Student-Centered Communicative Activities

#2: Famous Family Photo Album

You are a member of a famous family. Make a photo album. Include a photo of each member of your family. Tell us three things about each family member.

Digital versions work nicely for this. Students can narrate slides or provide written text.

#3: Interesting Family Member

This activity is a little more advanced (level 3+) and high interest.

Create a few simple questions in your target language asking for information about a member of their family that they did not necessarily know. I suggest using the equivalent of the word "interesting" in your target language. You might create an option for them to also find out something new about a family member they know well. Students will get an answer to these simple questions and share with the class in the target language.

Some students will talk about how they can't think of anything that the class would find interesting. They will likely learn something interesting about someone in their family that is very interesting indeed and be excited to share this with the class. Students will often learn things about their family that they did not know before and get TL speaking practice as well.

Consider having students write this as an essay or letter.

#4: Family Role Play

Brilliant Spanish teacher Rita Jimenez has a fun, low-prep, high-interest activity for beginners.

Split your class into families (think groups of 4–5+ ideally). Each student plays a member of that family.

One of the challenges in languages in learning to talk about families is the different vocabulary to describe each relationship. Some languages, such as Korean, have completely different words for "younger sister" and "older sister." For this reason, a lot of practice is necessary for students to really be able to talk about their families. Each student will need to practice the different words to describe their relationship to each different person.

After families have been formed, establish the criteria to work on during the practice/rehearsal period. For example, the student must introduce each family member, include a greeting, include one thing they like about each person, etc. The power in this activity is this practice and repetition as they prepare to introduce their family to the class, as well as whatever other tasks they will be completing.

Add in fun props to raise interest and engagement levels. Think things like baby bottles, ties, wigs, and thrift store clothes.

#5: Class Families

Organizing classes into families for a period of time is a way to create flexible and dynamic groupings as well as build community.

A note about exploring families: give students some choices. This can be a sensitive and loaded topic. Additionally, every family is different. Some are a child and parent; some are huge and multi-generational. There may be aspects individuals don't want to discuss, and choice could not be more important for this topic. Activities like Famous Family Photo Album allow for some choice in what to reveal or simply a fun way to imagine being a part of a famous family.

In some cultures, it is customary to stay with parents until marriage. In others, moving away at a much younger age is seen as perfectly acceptable. There are also many rich opportunities for comparing and contrasting cultures with this particular topic.

Weather and Seasons

These activities make for engaging sub plans or core lessons for days when you're exhausted (they happen). If you've taught beginners, you know that the amount of time they can spend on a single activity is short. These types of activities allow for students to showcase their creativity as well as practice what they are learning.

Starting with authentic, in-context, meaningful input allows for students to naturally acquire the target language.

#1: Consider displaying current weather reports from TL sources. Make it interactive by asking and answering questions based on the report. You might even provide students with a TL weather site, such as Metro France. List places and assign students to research the weather for the week and share. This also builds cultural competence.

Provide students with access to the vocabulary that they'll need to do the following mini projects. This might be their text or co-building a list with students.

#2: Doodle Mini-Project or Slide Show

- ◆ The student makes/finds a picture for each season.
- ◆ The student includes the months that belong to that season.
- ◆ The student writes the weather for that season.
- ◆ The student writes three activities that they do during each season.
- ◆ The student writes at least two sentences about what they like and dislike about each season.
- ◆ The student draws (or finds) at least 15 items (total) and labels them in the target language.

With the slide show option, students can narrate, record, and create a short video.

#3: Weather Reports

The student gives a weather report in the target language. Provide specific criteria that must be reported. TL websites provide the backdrop needed as well as visual prompts for speaking.

Each student selects a city from the TL culture. The student mentions three types of weather in the target language. The student only speaks the target language.

#4: Packing
This is a simple project that allows students to review common vocabulary for activities as well as clothing.

Have students select places in the TL culture. They should find ten activities to do in their chosen place.

Based on the research that they have done on the weather and the activities they found, they should "pack" for the weather. Using folded paper as an imaginary suitcase, they draw (photos or clip art work nicely, too) their selected items, labeling them in the target language. They can decorate their suitcase and review autobiographical information (i.e., *My name is...*, address, contact information, etc.).

Students can also include their itinerary, written in the target language.

Home

#1: A tour of my house.
Polyglot Benny Lewis offers tours of where he lives in different languages.

Option A: Give us a video tour of your house while you talk about it in your target language.

Option B: Take photos. Put each photo in a Google slide (or search Google images). Record your presentation.

(Remember that if it isn't really *your* house, we won't know!)

#2 Dream House
Have students draw their dream house, labeling all rooms and furniture.

- The student draws their dream house.
- The student labels the rooms.
- The student decorates the house and labels the furniture.
- The student writes two sentences describing the house.

72 ◆ Student-Centered Communicative Activities

- ◆ The student writes ten sentences describing what the house has.
- ◆ The student hands in a project that is neat and legible.

Do this as a drawing or as a presentation.

#3: Create simple origami dream houses and label them in the target language. There are many great tutorials available on YouTube.

#4: Students create Pinterest boards, captioning their finds in the target language. Students read one another's boards and leave comments in the target language.

Shopping

#1: Do My Shopping

"I need your help. Please work with your group to help me furnish my house."

Use the online stores below. Find and paste each item below with your group. Each accurate "purchase" is one point.

Je cherche…

- ◆ la table de nuit
- ◆ le canapé
- ◆ l'étagère
- ◆ le lit
- ◆ la commode
- ◆ la télévision
- ◆ l'armoire
- ◆ le micro-onde
- ◆ la cuisine/la cuisinière
- ◆ le réfrigérateur/le frigo
- ◆ la baignoire
- ◆ l'inodore
- ◆ le lavabo
- ◆ le lave-vaisselle
- ◆ la table
- ◆ la chaise

- ◆ le canapé
- ◆ le tapis
- ◆ la porte
- ◆ le miroir
- ◆ le tableau
- ◆ le coussin
- ◆ la lampe

This is fun to do in groups. While the task itself is not authentic, it is a great way to expose students to authentic resources.

#2: Shopping Transactions/Dialogues

Market/shopping activities in TL countries provide students with excellent opportunities for communication in all modes, as well as experience in building cultural competence.

I suggest introducing the task/theme with authentic input. Here are some examples that come to mind to help you find the right one for your language and level that can be found online:

- ◆ websites for department stores, such as Galeries Lafayettes
- ◆ videos of flea markets in Paris
- ◆ markets in Mexico
- ◆ souks
- ◆ German Christmas markets
- ◆ fish market in Tokyo
- ◆ international eBay/Amazon sites.

Expose students to these places with authentic input (a quick search) and/or display these sites, making the discussion communicative and interactive. Create (perhaps through Language Experience Approach or via a handout) a resource of the language they need to complete the task.

The student buys and sells goods at a market and/or their eBay shop.

Write a dialogue of at least 15 lines using the language to buy and sell at a market and/or your "listings" on your eBay shop.

The market and in-store shopping activities would be interactive speaking and listening activities.

The eBay activity would be a writing/presentational task. The "transaction" might be a written exchange between buyer and seller. This can also be writing an item description.

Clothing

Teaching clothing makes for engaging lessons that allow for communication in all modes. Difficult grammatical concepts can be embedded, often making for an authentic context to learn and master. Fashion shows, dress-up activities, and activities from art provide opportunities to acquire language and build cultural competence. Some additional ideas:

#1: Collect/Scavenger Hunt
This is similar to the shopping activities previously described. Use simple lists of vocabulary. Put them in teams and give them the list, and students then collect/doodle the items. They create a relevant active world language reading lesson.

More advanced students can create lists that they give to others. For example, they might make a list of clothing they want someone to buy. This is interactive and fun.

In this activity, students will go "shopping" for you. They must visit the following stores listed at the web address and link to items from those stores. You can assign this in groups (recommended). Students can draw doodles to show comprehension and their "purchases." The first group to accurately find your items wins.

> "I need your help. Please work with your group and do my shopping." Use the online stores below. Find and paste each item below with your group. Tiendas de ropa en línea:
>
> - www.zara.com/ic
> - https://shop.mango.com/es
> - www.elcorteingles.es

Busco...

- una camiseta roja de mangas cortas
- una camisa a rayas
- zapatos negros
- pantalones cortos verdes
- una falda larga
- zapatillas
- calcetines blancos
- traje
- gafas de sol
- un suéter azul
- ropa interior
- un chaleco
- vaqueros
- medias
- un vestido
- un cinturon
- una blusa blanca
- botas de cuero
- un gorro
- un abrigo
- un sombrero
- una chaqueta gris
- una corbata
- un impermeable
- una bufanda

A richer variation on this is similar to packing for the weather. Provide students with specific tasks (i.e., I need a dress for my niece's wedding, skiing in Bariloche, dinner in Buenos Aires, etc.). They must shop specifically for your needs.

TPR shopping activities: Provide a flyer (easily available online) and have students select ten items to buy. Make it simpler by reducing the number of items. Make it more advanced by having them explain their purchases. I love to use branded bags from TL countries whenever possible to add in more culture.

#2: Dream Wardrobe

This is a variation on shopping and makes it more personal and high interest.

The student creates a Pinterest board or another type of presentation with at least 15 different clothing items.

The student writes a description for each item that they choose. The description is at least three sentences for each item. Each description has correct noun/adjective agreement.

Having props on hand for clothing activities is a must. Old clothes—the odder and more varied the better. Your classroom is a great place for clothing people no longer wear. This can be yours, your family members', donations, and thrift store/charity shop finds. Add a clothesline, clothespins, and old magazines for even more low-prep, high-interest activities to learn to talk about clothing in a new language.

Menus and Restaurants

Simple instructions here. Students create a short menu (you decide the criteria). Provide them with essential words and phrases to order in a restaurant.

Once they are done with their menus, let them practice being the server and customer. The quiz is the dramatization.

A few variations on this classic:

#1: Target Language Restaurants

Assign your class different places in your TL culture. They must research two restaurants there and bookmark the menus. They then select one of the menus to be their menu for their restaurant dramatization. Students are assigned different TL places and design menus based on the dishes they found.

#2: Dream Restaurant/Food Truck

Students create their own dream restaurants or food trucks designed around their favorite foods. They can also create food truck concepts or grand menus for a special occasion. The idea is to allow them to infuse their personal passions, preferences, and talents to produce high-quality work and acquire language at the same time.

#3: Delivery

Many food delivery services are operating around the world and have websites in different languages. These sites provide high-quality comprehensible input with photos. Have students find meals for a day and share them with the class.

Make these more advanced by requiring there to be a complaint and resolution. Some ideas:

- ◆ Order was never delivered.
- ◆ Order had items missing.
- ◆ Food was cold.

Writing a complaint letter is the perfect extension of this activity. Having a collection of plastic foods and TL food containers or labels on hand can serve as props or be used for low-prep games. Your classroom might also have taste tests (post surveys in the target language) or occasions to share TL dishes.

The Time

Learning to tell time in the target language can be difficult. I recommend a lot of comprehensible input without any explanation for a long time before you do any explicit teaching. Keep it short and easy to understand. Some ideas:

#1: Expose students to schedules online in your target language (i.e., trains, buses, movies, television). Ask and answer questions about what you're displaying. Alternatively, print them out and have them find specific things (i.e., what time a specific program is on).

#2: Label a clock in your room with the TL chunks needed to say the time in your target language. See the clock in the Templates section to personalize and display.

78 ◆ Student-Centered Communicative Activities

#3: Time bingo. Use the calling cards (digital works well) and a lot of repetition to provide input. Allow students to take over being the caller when they are ready.

#4: TPR is perfect for learning to tell time. Get clocks with movable hands. Some teachers have students make these if their district does not purchase them. Create "hands" from cardstock and add to the classroom display model. See the template to create one for your students.

#5: Write out your school schedule and times in your target language. List classes and activities in the target language. Have students fill in these charts. Use these as listening and speaking prompts.

#6: Show and tell the time, modeling, asking, and answering the question. Students will chime in when they are ready.

#7: Hula hoops are a great investment for language teachers and serve many purposes (i.e., colored to understand gender of nouns, giant Venn diagrams, TPR categorizations).

For time, tape them to the board. Divide students into groups. Using their books, they write the times that you say. If you have whiteboards, more students can participate, writing the times that you say to demonstrate understanding.

#6: After they have had exposure, assign a short project for them to apply what they learned. Use your textbook or a handout to help them complete the project.

The student chooses eight different times of the day and writes them in the target language on paper OR creates narrated slides, including times when they do different activities.

The student includes which part of the day it is.

The student includes a picture of the activity they normally do at that time. For example, *I go to French class at ten thirty in the morning.*

Students might write out their school schedules to talk about different times of the day as well.

Mini Tasks

Many of the experiences that we design for our learners are, of course, not authentic. However, having these experiences helps to build communicative skills. They allow students to experience conversational language without the pressure of a real exchange—a critical first step.

Some high-interest mini experiences:

#1: Gatherings

It is vital to expose students to some cultural norms of your target language. This might be understanding the difference between the importance of a name day in some cultures (i.e., Greek), music, and how birthdays are celebrated (i.e., food, customs, etc.).

The student creates a dramatization of at least four scenes or frames in which a holiday or another gathering (e.g., a birthday) is celebrated. The drama that the student creates is in the form of a video, storyboard, recording, poster, comic strip, or short play.

The story includes the following elements:

- a greeting
- someone asking another a question about the special occasion/gathering
- someone answering that question
- ask and answer about ages
- appropriate wishes
- thank you
- take leave.

OR:

Create a card to bring to the gathering for someone important to you or a classmate (draw names).

The context also allows for some type of inclusion of a cultural practice/product and conversation practice.

Some other contexts to use to teach using this method include:

- a holiday
- a trip
- a great day
- a bad day
- getting a pet
- ordering in a restaurant

80 ◆ Student-Centered Communicative Activities

- ◆ talking about your house
- ◆ talking about the weather
- ◆ talking about sports
- ◆ illustrating a recipe.

Short Simulations and Dramatizations

A quick note about the difference between the two: a simulation is unscripted, and a dramatization is scripted. For Novice/A-range learners, a lot of support is necessary to do a simulation, so it may, in reality, be more like a dramatization. Either way, they are both effective for practicing real-life communicative situations.

Use short simulations and dramatizations for many situations regarding talking about health (i.e., pharmacy, nurse's office), travel, meeting and greeting for the first time, or any topic that requires students to engage in a short conversation that would not be a natural task in your class.

It is a good experience for all to build the task together. What would people do and say in this situation? List it out. Then brainstorm the TL words, chunks, and phrases that the students will use. You may want to do it like this the first time and save this work for future years.

Your list might have things like greetings, commands telling what the speaker must do (i.e., give advice about health).

If you choose to prepare in advance, hand out the prompts and go over language needed with students. Students can also find their own words and phrases.

Allow them to practice over and over before performing this with the class.

Have students prepare all of the roles in the simulation/dramatization and perform repeatedly with students playing all roles.

Fake Texts

#1: Fake Texts for Input

Create fake text activities using fake text generators. These are easily found online. While I believe the purpose of their invention might have been for more nefarious purposes than ours, they are still very useful for practicing this very useful and ubiquitous communication method.

Be intentional with what you create, using it as an opportunity to provide comprehensible input.

After comprehension is clear, move on to creation. It is a great way to work in different modes of communication and learn current TL text language and abbreviations.

Generate comprehension questions. Make it low prep by doing this as an interactive activity and creating the questions with the students.

Here is an example in Spanish:

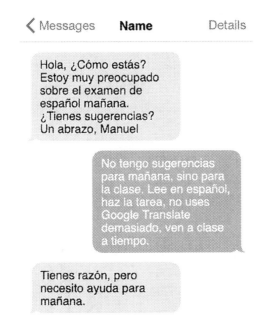

#2/Extension: Create Fake Texts

Some language to tell people what to do:

- Estudia = study
- Ve = go
- Habla = talk
- Mira = look at
- Ten = have

82 ◆ Student-Centered Communicative Activities

- ◆ Pon = put
- ◆ Lee = read
- ◆ Escribe = write
- ◆ Envia = send
- ◆ Di = tell

Write ten lines (at least), including TL characters (use "insert special characters" in Google Docs or write them in by hand if creating a poster). Include text abbreviations.

Fake Text Abbreviations in Spanish

abreviatura	español	inglés
tkm/tqm	Te quiero mucho	I love you
k	que	what
ntp	No te preocupes	Don't worry
pq/pk/xp	¿Por qué?	Why?
tlj	te lo juro	I swear
npn	No pasa nada	No big deal
fds	fin de semana	weekend
grrr	enfadado	angry
mdi	me da igual	it's the same to me
kn	quien	who
msj	mensaje	message
pti	para tu información	FYI
TQI/TKI	tengo que irme	I have to go
mxo	mucho	A lot
hl	hasta luego	see you later
aki	aquí	here
bs	besos	kisses
a2	adiós	bye
gpi	gracias por invitar	thanks for the invite

Students may want to collaborate on their responses, making it even more interactive.

Doodles, Sketches, Drawings, and Short Writing Activities

One of my favorite tips to learn a new language that I love to share is the power of doodling. I consider it a powerful form of journaling.

Student-Centered Communicative Activities ◆ 83

Journaling daily will have a great impact on fluency. Keep some form of a personal journal for studies. It can be part of the task notebook, communication journal, or something separate. Do whatever you need to develop the language that you want students to learn.

Consider using themed vocabulary from a traditional textbook or a workbook of themed vocabulary. While it is not time spent on authentic communication with another person in the target language, it can be a great way to get some input and build skills during time that would otherwise not be spent in the target language.

I hope this gives you some ideas on how to use these for low-prep, highly engaging activities. I also recommend assigning vocabulary from a textbook and allowing students to draw their own scenes or illustrated flash cards. It is a great way to learn new words on their own and enjoy doing so.

- ◆ **A Salad:** Draw a salad. Using a themed vocabulary list, label all of the fruits and vegetables you include. Next, use the visual to write about your salad in as much detail as possible.
- ◆ **My Body/My Face:** Sketch out a person. Label everything that you can. Use the illustration as a prompt to write about yourself.
- ◆ **A Person Made of Food:** This is a fun one that requires some thought and engagement in vocabulary. Basically, you create a person made of drawings (or clipart) of foods. You then create a key using the names of the body and face parts and the food vocabulary you used to represent the face and body. You then use your creation as a prompt to write as detailed a description as possible. This also gives you an opportunity to learn about different types of foods from the target culture. Up the proficiency range of this activity by adding questions about the character's background and past to include in the response.
- ◆ **Portrait:** Draw a picture of yourself or another person. Label everything you can. Next, write as much as you can about the person.

- **Where I Live:** This is quite self-explanatory. Sketch out where you live. Label everything you can. Write about where you live.
- *Variation:* Do the same but for your dream house or where someone else lives.
- **Likes and Dislikes:** I love this for basic lists of vocabulary. You can categorize activities, classes, places in the world, foods, drinks, artists, music genres, books—anything you can imagine. Use the lists to write a paragraph.
- **Schedules:** Write out your daily schedule, a school schedule, a train schedule, or a movie schedule.
- **Dates:** Write out important dates. These can be holidays, important dates in your life, important dates in the culture of the target language, or birthdays of family and friends. Place them on a timeline and write about why each is important.
- **An Alien (or Monster):** Design your alien or monster. Use body parts from different images to create an original being. Label the parts. Describe this creation in as much detail as possible.
- **My Garden:** Take a photo or sketch your yard or garden. Label all of the items that you include. Write about what you see, and talk about what you do there and anything you would like to do there in the future.
- **My Family:** I particularly like this one, as one can keep this short and simple by only including immediate family or it can be turned into an informative, extended project. Using photos or drawings and create a family tree. Write about each person as well as their relationship to you. Including extended family can serve as a reason to learn advanced vocabulary to talk about family as well as a context to work in the past tense.
- **Nature:** Draw or get photos of beautiful scenes of nature. These can become great stimuli for learning and using descriptive words and vocabulary for talking about nature and geography. It can become a cultural experience when the photos come from the target culture.

Student-Centered Communicative Activities ◆ 85

- **My School:** This topic has so many possibilities. You can talk about any school that you have attended. The classes you took, liked, and disliked make for rich stimuli for writing and vocabulary development. The people you interact with or have interacted with in the past can be writing topics.

This list is in no way exhaustive. The purpose is to get you thinking about how students can get working with new words in your target language easily and in an enjoyable way.

Here are some additional prompts that don't require drawing.

- **Hobbies:** Describe your favorite hobby or activity in your own words.
- **Dream vacation:** Write about your dream vacation destination and what you would do there.
- **Earlier in my life:** Share a funny or interesting story from your childhood.
- **Superpowers:** Imagine you are a superhero. Describe your powers and how you would save the day.
- **My future:** Write a letter to your future self. What do you hope to achieve in the next five years? There are fun apps that allow people to write these and then send them at a later date, too.
- **The best day:** Describe the perfect day from morning to night. Include details about what you would eat, where you would go, and who you would be with.
- **Trip:** Describe a memorable moment from a recent trip or outing with your friends or family.
- **Things I love:** Write a list of things that make you happy and explain why they bring you joy.
- **A great day off:** Describe your ideal day off from school or work. What would you do to relax and have fun?
- **Foods I love:** Share a recipe for your favorite dish and explain why you enjoy cooking or eating it.
- **Animals:** Imagine you could talk to any animal. Which animal would you choose and what would you ask?

86 ◆ Student-Centered Communicative Activities

- ◆ **Great stories:** Describe your favorite book or movie and why you enjoy it.
- ◆ **Letters:** Write a letter to someone you admire and explain why you look up to them.
- ◆ **A future place:** Describe a place you would love to visit in the future and what you hope to see and do there.

Google Translate and Artificial Intelligence

Many of us language teachers think about online translators a lot. The fact is they are getting better and better all the time. Google Translate started scanning documents translated by humans years ago when they started. It also still asks for feedback from users. These norms make them more and more accurate and reliable all the time. With that said, we know that while we celebrate the access available to language now, we want students to build their own skills. I suggest doing writing assessments by hand to help build those skills. We want them to know the difference between a good translation and the incorrect ones these tools sometimes produce.

As professionals, we have the language skills to use these tools to help us save time. Don't feel shy about using the translate document function on things like graphic organizers. You'll likely need to edit, check, revise and cite to ensure that it was done correctly. These tools can save you loads of time.

AI is making tremendous strides all the time. Use it in conjunction with your language skills to create TL experiences and input. Consider using AI tools to create experiences for learners, such as exit tickets, writing prompts, and TL reading selections, questions, and answers. The prompts on superpowers and animals were generated with the help of AI (in this case, ChatGPT). With light editing, they could be easily adapted to make them useful. Use your language skills and knowledge to check for accuracy and edit.

Avatar videos and text-to-voice tools can take these AI-generated texts and create listening comprehension activities, providing input and saving precious time.

References

Benny Lewis. "Polyglot Tour of Apartment: Benny Lewis in New York." YouTube, 3 May 2016, www.youtube.com/watch?v=K_mGPIPOP5Q&t=87s. Accessed 12 December 2023.

Tonni art and craft. "How to Make a Beautiful Paper House/DIY Miniature Paper House." YouTube, 14 June 2020, www.youtube.com/watch?v=Dcpv3oaHq8s. Accessed 12 December 2023.

5

Communicative and Research Projects

In addition to developing the ability to communicate in the target language and interculturality, we want students to develop the twenty-first-century skills of critical thinking, collaboration, digital and media literacy, resilience, flexibility, initiative, agency, and ethical reasoning as well. Language classes provide an ideal context to develop these skills with high-interest activities.

Cultural Research Projects

#1: History Reports
Offer a couple of simple activities to learn about history and current events in the target language.

Offer students a menu of current events, history, or culture (whatever you are studying). Tell them that they have to make a presentation that is no longer than three slides (including citations) to tell us about what they researched. This keeps

DOI: 10.4324/9781032622507-9

answers focused and manageable in terms of time, and forces learners to only share the most salient points.

This same technique can also be used for art. Select an artist from your TL country, or from a specific museum, and ask students to create a presentation. Each student must tell the class a few things about their painting. This is a great way to get exposure to art and practice TL culture and language at the same time.

#2: Compare and Contrast

Cultural research projects are great because they can be adapted to any theme or topic and proficiency level. An example of a short presentation can be a simple 20-minute project in which students fill in a Venn diagram on the similarities and differences between simple, everyday aspects of culture.

An example would be school schedules in their country and their target language. A country's foods or holidays are other high-interest examples. The research and diagram serve as speaking prompts.

Students can research an aspect of culture that interests them. Give them some choices (i.e., a dance, a book, a person) related to your theme but keep the criteria succinct and clear (i.e., 5–7 slides, sentences, facts). Let them narrate out loud or present a recorded version.

As students advance, they can start making comparisons between cultures. For example:

- ◆ holidays
- ◆ families
- ◆ clothing
- ◆ school
- ◆ foods
- ◆ economies.

90 ◆ Communicative and Research Projects

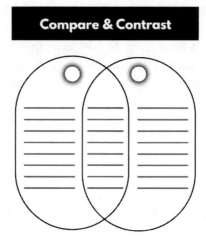

Compare and Contrast

Compare and Contrast Two Similar Ideas, Practices, or Things in the TL Culture and the Student's Native Culture

High-Interest Compare and Contrast

Create high-interest compare and contrast prompts. Some examples:

- Compare and contrast the Kardashians and a TL royal family.
- Compare and contrast Starbucks in your country and a TL country.
- Compare and contrast real estate sites in your country and a TL country.
- Compare and contrast average ages when people leave home in their country and TL country.
- Compare and contrast domiciles/homes in their country/ TL country.

Through languages, I have learned about more holidays and am fascinated by learning about their history and origins. After learning about the history of Halloween and Samhain (Celtic New Year), I see deeper connections and opportunities for cultural and linguistic immersion through exploring topics like All Saints' and el Día de los Muertos (triple Venn diagram in Templates) and winter holidays. These activities provide high-interest topics and contexts for developing language proficiency.

Argue and Persuade

As students hit the intermediate level and can create with language, they can start building argumentative and persuasive skills. The key to this is to select high-interest content and topics. Some examples:

- dress codes and school uniforms
- school schedules that meet more often or schedules in different countries
- vegetarianism versus eating meat
- minimum age for driving or seeing certain films

92 ◆ Communicative and Research Projects

- living at home versus away for university
- studying for a degree versus a trade or other profession
- starting a business versus working for someone else
- plastic surgery versus natural appearance
- bullfighting: culture or just plain wrong?
- social media versus no social media for teens
- phones in school: yes or no?

As students advance in their TL skills:

- Should governments provide universal healthcare?
- Should the use of plastic utensils and bags be prohibited?
- Is online education more beneficial than traditional education?
- Is homeschooling better than traditional education?
- Should the voting age be lowered below 18?
- Does technology in the classroom help or harm students?
- Has your experience with standardized tests been beneficial to you? Why or why not?

These are just a few examples to get you started. Provide high-interest topics, access to authentic sources to support their arguments, and help with the language they need to make their argument and build proficiency in the target language.

An easy way to organize this is with a T-chart. These T-charts are great for Language Experience Approach activities, where you build the sides of an argument and provide students with input that they can use to express their opinions while developing the you-level skill of getting people to take a course of action, accept something as true, or adopt a different point of view.

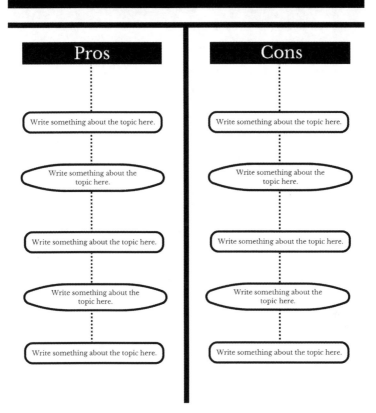

T Chart

94 ◆ Communicative and Research Projects

Name _____ Date _____	

1. Read/listen to a source.
2. Read/listen to another source.
3. Choose your opinion.
4. Find evidence from the sources and fill in the organizer.
5. Write 75–100 words.
6. Cite your sources.

Question: do you agree or not?	
Yes	No

For both argumentative work and compare and contrast, consider handing out Post-its. Allow students to write opinions and thoughts and place them on a large board that you have made. Share opinions and discuss. All of the input that students will have before actually creating a product will make it significantly easier for them. It also requires more than one mode of communication.

A note about high-interest topics: the more passionate we are about a topic, the more interested we are. The more interested we are, the more we will want to engage, which is important to keep in mind as you plan.

One such topic for Spanish teachers is bullfighting. The topic provides such a rich context to compare and contrast cultures, attitudes, and opinions. Many people believe it is barbaric and will want to acquire the language necessary to express that opinion. Some people think it is an important example of culture and attitudes, both past and present.

In order to do these types of activities, students will need some knowledge about the basics of the topic that you are covering. In the past, I have written about this topic and had it narrated as well as providing some clips and photos of the practice to provide an overview. The visuals helped illustrate that there were not a lot of spectators in the case I shared, showing its waning attendance rates. This can be evidence to use in an argument against the practice.

Selecting sources from varying points of view provides even more input and opportunities to develop counterclaims and structures for concession (i.e. although, even though), where an opposing point of view is acknowledged, showing that multiple points of view have been considered—an Advanced/C-range skill. Using the example of bullfighting again, showing students that there has been government investment in training bullfighters in the past might provide them with a context to acknowledge that while it is a long-standing tradition, it is difficult to find people to train to keep it alive. There are also many protests. The simple fact that it is outlawed in Cataluña and their main *plaza de toros* is now a market can help a learner develop an argument. These same materials might be used for the opposing point of view.

Selecting topics will depend on your level, theme, topic, and culture. And when I say culture, I am not just referring to your TL culture but your particular school and classroom. Even broaching certain topics might be viewed as advocating for a particular opinion. This will vary for each and every teacher. Some tips as you build your repertoire:

1. YouTube playlists are a great place to organize and curate authentic videos to use as a source and input. You can keep them unlisted as you decide if and how you might use them. Documents with links work, too.
2. Authentic articles are the best. I suggest saving them in documents where you curate materials for similar themes.
3. If Google searches for authentic articles don't yield promising results, consider AI to write a quick report on a topic to get started. Check your facts and have it create a glossary.

Travel

Travel and all that we can learn from it is an often-used context in our language teaching. Here are a few activities to build skills using travel in your classes.

#1: Postcards

Use postcards often in your language teaching. You may have picked many up during your travels over the years. They are so easy to make with free photo sites now, too.

Write everyone's names on a small slip of paper. Write places from all over the world (or TL countries) on other slips. Place all of these slips in two bags. Students select a name and a place. They write a postcard from the place they "visited" to the person they selected. Give them specific requirements based on what we are working on. For example, have them research food, sites, apartments, and excursions from the place they chose. They will need to do research and include accurate information in their postcard.

Mail delivery day is fun when everyone gets their postcard.

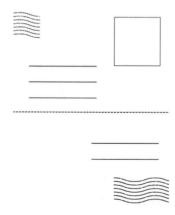

Postcard Template

#2: Write postcards in your target language, or have a native-speaking contact write them. Consider themes from your course and high-frequency vocabulary. Deliver to students, and use them as a foundation for a response. They can serve as a great source of comprehensible input. Do a digital version of your cards to use year after year.

Travel Realia

Realia is a flexible and engaging tool for learning and language teaching. Some ways to incorporate it into your classes:

#1: Create a scrapbook of realia from your target language for your class library.

#2: Have students do a scavenger hunt to find realia covering specific things (i.e., menus, tickets, advertisements, telephone numbers, etc.).

#3: Require the use of realia in projects, dramatizations, and role plays.

#4: Create a reading assignment from your realia. These are extremely useful and practical because these are what people will encounter in the TL country when there.

Many teachers say that they are using free online templates to generate fake boarding passes, too. It's fun stuff and conducive to speaking activities. An editable template can be found in the digital resources.

Boarding Pass Template

#5: Faraway Places

Print out some maps of countries or cities and place them in a bag. The students will draw one place each.

98 ◆ Communicative and Research Projects

Students will research ten things/customs/meals (or anything you choose) from the place they drew. They will write a letter telling the class about their home country/city, including the photos they found. Read these to the class and hang them on the wall.

This works best in a lower intermediate level but can be adapted to any other. Select any place you choose (even your own home).

#6: Plan a Trip

Students can make their own Pinterest accounts, and they can all collaborate on secret boards. Alternatively, make a collaborative Google slide.

This is great fun. For example, if you teach French, your French class can collaborate on boards planning a trip, virtual or real, to France. They can find restaurants and stores and hotels and transportation. More advanced French students can use French keywords; all of your students can be required to comment on everyone else's Pins in the target language.

Not planning a trip with your class? The secret boards could be used for any theme that you're teaching such as the house or food in the target language—it's great fun. Do on paper, Canva, or a slide presentation.

#7: Airbnb

Rental sites provide many opportunities to not only provide TL input for students but also see properties in TL places. With some of these global brands, their technology will display your page in your language based on your IP. Consider ensuring students are in your TL default or taking screenshots of interesting properties in TL countries to serve as examples and input. Co-create with students what the outcome should be for their own Airbnb listing.

Communicative and Research Projects ◆ 99

Real-Life Task Practice

Make up scenarios to practice real life in the target language as much as possible with more simulations, role plays, and dramatizations. They provide great context for getting experience in a much less threatening way than real life might be.

#1: Job Interview

One such activity is a job interview. Start with some online ads for jobs from your target language. I am loving employment sites with different language versions. Your students might search for a summer job in Paris. You might print these out and post them for students to select from. This then becomes a reading activity.

Once students have identified a "job" they might be interested in, they write a letter of interest. You can conduct the interview yourself. Invite a native speaker to conduct the interview if possible.

Give the students the papers beforehand with all the criteria needed. Consider simple questions you might encounter in a job interview and tailor them to allow you to recycle language from your course or previous courses. This might be basic biographical information (i.e. your name, education, etc.). Add specifics you want students to practice such as structures, vocabulary or tasks (i.e. ask questions). Next, hand out the interview questions for students to prepare. (See the following box.)

Set up the "office" in another location. The students practice each role as they are waiting for their turn.

> You will participate in a simulated job interview with a native speaker. She is the owner of a company that helps place people seeking jobs with available positions in different places.
>
> Be prepared to answer the following questions:
>
> ◆ What is your name?
> ◆ What position interests you? Why?

100 ◆ Communicative and Research Projects

> ◆ Tell me about your qualities, abilities, skills, and knowledge.
> ◆ Have you filled out an application?
> ◆ Do you have experience?
> ◆ Do you have references? (Give the interviewer at least one reference. Include how you know each person. Be sure to tell them how to get in touch with the person.)
> ◆ Do you have any questions? (Ask at least five questions about the job to the interviewer.)
>
> You will not be able to bring your papers during the interview, so be sure to prepare your answers at home and take full advantage of the practice period before the interview.

Consider which language points and vocabulary you want the learners to master as you craft your questions. Do they need to use the descriptive words from your text? Will they need commands? Formal language? This type of project is a great opportunity to include difficult concepts or recycle grammar and vocabulary.

For Intermediate and Advanced level learners, consider some fun variations to create a more linguistically challenging task:

◆ Hand out slips to students telling them to do specific things during the interview (i.e., yawn). Allow the interviewer to provide feedback.

◆ Provide feedback reports for students in the target language. A native-speaking guest may be willing to help with this. Alternatively, write a paragraph or so for each student. A low-prep tip would be to draft out some standard responses beforehand of common errors you anticipate (or use AI help). Copy and paste feedback, adding some individualized feedback to hand out for more language input.

◆ Students can also prepare real job interview materials, such as a resumé and cover letter (great for native speakers, too).

Some other contexts to create these types of experiences:

#2: Specialized topics of your expertise and, even better, a guest speaker. Think things like specialized collections a guest might have (i.e., butterflies) or knowledge (i.e., their job). Students do some research in advance and craft questions for the guest lecture.

#3: Special personal interest projects. Students might love music, sports, or dance. They research specific people (i.e., an athlete). You might edit them and send questions to the person's website contact (from your account). These famous people may respond. Either way, students experience communication in more than one mode and engage with TL people.

Depending on your access, find native speakers in the community to come to your class. Keep it low prep by having students do the research, write the letters and questions, and you do the contacting. It might be a native-speaking nurse who can come to your class during your health unit and teach words and phrases to beginners and provide an immersive lecture for Intermediate and Advanced students.

#3: Your classroom theater

Using what you are already working on, rearrange your room to mimic the environment. Practice and complete the task. Some ideas:

- airplane
- talk show
- radio show
- movie theater
- market
- doctor's office
- restaurant
- Greek theater with Chorus, à la Dr. Rassius (great for songs)
- theater for dialogues
- café in Paris

More Engaging Projects

Here are a few ideas for Intermediate and Advanced students to recycle grammar and vocabulary, build skills, and enjoy doing so.

#1: Imagine you are lost in a foreign country and create a conversation with a local in which you ask for directions to various places using your target language. Write out each person's lines.

#2: Draw a map of a made-up city using the target language's words for places, such as streets and buildings. What would you name a park? A school?

#3: Design a dream outfit. Describe it using the target language's words for different pieces of clothing and accessories. Use words in the target language to bring it to life.

#4: Create a conversation between a tourist and a local shopkeeper using only emojis to represent the phrases in your target language. Create a key to decode the conversation.

#5: Write a news article about an animal or celebrity in your target language. Add photos.

#6: Create a comic strip or short story (see Storyboard).

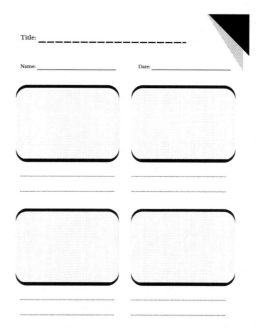

Storyboard

SECTION 5

The majority of class time is spent doing activities that build communication skills. Communicative activities that involve speaking, listening, reading, writing, and culture are used to build fluency in each.

6

Reading

Regular reading is one of the most effective ways to acquire/ learn a new language. Dr. Stephen Krashen wrote a paper in 2017 titled "Polyglots and the Comprehension Hypothesis." The subjects of his study each spoke more than 15 languages. They both cite extensive reading as a major factor in their success.

Many teachers have FVR (Free Voluntary Reading) time and/or dedicated reading assignments regularly in their classes. A class library is an invaluable asset. Curating target language reading and creating a routine in which students read regularly helps engage them in target language input. Vocabulary and grammar can be acquired, completely in context.

I'm a certified reading teacher, kindergarten teacher, as well as a language teacher and have gone through the process of building literacy with people in their native language. When we teach people how to read, we first learn to read. Only after this can we read to learn. At the end of the day, when we start learning how to read, we're learning what the language we speak looks like—visual representations of our languages. When we're learning that, we also learn a lot of things at the same time. We learn directionality, how to use cues to scan the page, pictures, known words, sight words, and decoding.

For example, learning how to read the word *the* could be very confusing based on your emerging knowledge of the alphabet, sounds, and what certain combinations of words sound like together.

DOI: 10.4324/9781032622507-11

When we select text for readers as they're learning how to read, we try to not make it too difficult or too easy. There's usually a range between 89/90% and 94%. That's a real sweet spot. It's not too easy and it's not too hard.

As we're learning how to read, we don't want it to be overwhelming (submersion). We don't want students to drown. We want them to be able to understand and really get something out of it without it being too easy.

USING READING TO LEARN
FOREIGN LANGUAGES

People learn languages by understanding messages (Krashen). Deep reading is a great way to understand messages.

LEARN TO READ
READ TO LEARN
Learning to read is learning what the language we speak looks like. We learn to read and then often read to learn.

89-94%

People learning to read should understand no less than 89% (too hard) of what they read and no more than 94% (too easy). Don't expect learners of a new language to understand what they read at these levels as they know far fewer words in the new language.

Traditional questions and answers are not enough to extract and retain vocabulary to use in real comprehension and communication.

ACTIVE READING

Pre-reading, scaffolding, support, active reading, multiple opportunities to dig deep for comprehension and communicative extension activities are necessary to understand, acquire language and develop strategies for reading in a foreign language.

Using Reading to Learn Foreign Languages

106 ◆ Reading

In an ideal world, we would have ready access to authentic readings that are high-interest, not too hard, but also not too easy. While there are resources out there, I think that the more realistic response in many cases is to provide learners with the tools to make reading comprehensible.

The challenge here is to connect these concepts to the concepts of people learning languages like the hyperpolyglots. Literacy skills are transferable. If you're an adult and you know how to read, then you can take a lot of shortcuts, but you're still going to experience all that frustration based on your level and know-ledge of other potential writing systems. It's not going to be like reading in your native language.

These activities require learners to read multiple times and interact deeply with the text. They create immersive experiences with the necessary support to lead to natural language acquisition.

Not being able to readily read in the target language contributes to some languages being significantly more diffi-cult than others. These teachers must dedicate time and focus to teaching vocabulary and what it looks like at the same time. There is often some rote repetition and traditional practice to build these skills.

Nonfiction

Nonfiction reading is the perfect activity if you want to learn something and work on your language skills at the same time, combining two goals. I did a whole lot of work with nonfiction to get up to a high level in Spanish using audio books. Basically, engage in interesting content in other languages. You'll need the language to understand the message, forcing you to work for comprehension.

Online news articles are a great way to do this. There are lots of things to read there, but I would also say a good source is Google News to learn in a new language. Once you have some of the basics down, go ahead and dig a bit deeper into reading to learn. Think about any topic you want to learn more about. It can be cooking. It can be history, mathematics, science, current events, or politics. You name it. Just do your reading in another language.

The challenge for teachers is finding material that is comprehensible (or can be made comprehensible) and high-interest, and can be used to create a communicative activity. The only way to do this is one step at a time to build a library of curated content that fits this criterion of being accessible and high-interest.

Strategies to Make Authentic and Difficult Target Language Text Comprehensible

Learning Other Scripts and Reading to Learn

To become literate, it is necessary to be able to both write and read. While our literacy skills are transferable, making it possible for us to use our reading strategies in new languages, we need to go back to the basics.

The very first step in learning how to write is to copy other writing. The activities you do when you are learning a new visual representation for language will be understanding and then copying. Some scripts are significantly easier to learn (i.e., Korean) for English speakers than others (i.e., Mandarin). Some portion of your time is going to be spent learning a new script if you teach one of those languages.

We learn to read before we read to learn. This applies to those of us learning another language, too. Dedicate some time to basic reading skills. This might mean only recognizing that in order to make reading an effective, non-tear-inducing, engaging, language acquisition/learning experience, you'll need to have patience and provide students strategies, time, grace, and space to make reading comprehensible.

Summaries

Write a summary of everything you read. Start with selecting a number of relevant facts, opinions, or descriptions from the selection. You might have them extract ten facts from the reading and then summarize in their own words using their extracts as input. Select the criteria and have them create something with what they have found in the reading.

Interesting Scenes

Students read and select interesting scenes to illustrate and describe. Use the scene as a speaking prompt to retell the story. Giant Post-its are great for this.

Mark up Text and Highlight

Mark all over what you are reading. Write in definitions, highlight, underline, make notes in the margins. Write as much as you can to make this incomprehensible text comprehensible. Read the selection several times and complete with an output activity.

This first set of tools involves low-tech things you can write with. Obviously, they must print out their reading. To the best of one's ability, write and mark up all over the text. Highlight and underline unknown words. Make notes in the margins.

Where we might be able to read something once or twice in our own language to get it, we might be reading it four and five times to really understand all that vocabulary and truly comprehend the piece in a new language. Maybe on the first sweep, we have to go through, mark it up, look up numerous words, and make notes on the text. I like using photocopies for this purpose, to go back and read it again, and then end with a writing activity. This is simply marking your paper up as much as you can so that the reader can walk away with a whole new set of vocabulary.

If that is not an option, use tiny post-it notes. If the book or selection is yours, do the same thing, using highlighters of different colors for different things. For a time, it's really about just digging deep into a text to get all the benefits of reading, without approaching it the same way one would doing pleasure reading in our first language.

Another way to do this as a beginner is to take a piece of paper, fold it in half, and cut out the middle. Place it over the text and write all over the margins to make the text comprehensible. If the selection is longer, do it as a jigsaw activity, assigning different sections to different groups. Make a gallery with the frames. Students should read others' frames. Finish the activity with individual summaries.

Questions

There's a reason a lot of textbooks have questions: they make reading active. The reader must go back and think about what was read and dig for the answers.

If it's a journalistic piece, ask: who, what, when, where, why? If it's a newspaper or a magazine article, answer in your journal.

In a class setting, make it interactive. Have pairs and groups create questions with answers that can only be found in the text for other pairs and groups. Then it becomes a speaking and listening activity as well. A variation of this can be to have pairs or groups create specific questions that are opinion-based for other groups.

Read with Others

Reading with others is one of the most powerful ways to learn a language. If you're reading on your own, mark up the text if that's possible. When students read with a partner, have them take turns reading out loud. It provides pronunciation practice and listening, too. Let them go back and forth, then do comprehension activities together. They're interacting with each other and the text. People are able to help each other problem-solve. It builds community, too.

Foreign language group reading for beginners works well. The threat of having to read in front of a group of people is gone.

When reading alone, marking up the text and saying things out loud is another way to get that practice.

SQ3R

In SQ3R (Survey Question, Read, Recall/Recite, Review), readers interact multiple times with a text. After surveying or scanning the selection to see what it might be about, the reader then composes questions. These might be questions made from the section headings, pictures, point of interest from the reading, or predictions. It tells them to look at the titles, the subtitles, and the photos. Those are things that readers do. What is this going to be about? Next, readers can create a question for each paragraph or heading (or whatever you deem appropriate), or three points of interest. Next, they read to answer the questions. The next step is to recall (or recite) by checking to see if the answers to the questions can be easily recalled. At the end, I like to write a summary to encourage more language acquisition. This can take something that's completely foreign to deep comprehension and language acquisition.

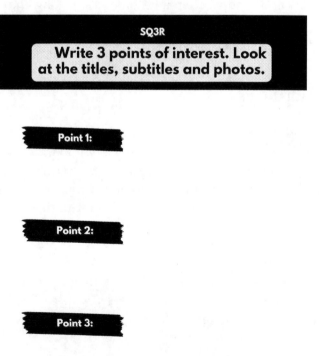

SQ3R 1

Reading ◆ 111

Write a question for each paragraph and its answer.

Questions	Answers

Write a summary:

SQ3R 2

My Character

Select one character from your reading and describe them in depth. Include their name, descriptions of their personality and physical traits, flaws, strengths, conflicts, relationships at work or school, and what others think of them.

My Character

Name:

Description:

Place of origin, age, likes and dislikes:

Family, friends, coworkers, acquiantances

Conflicts:

Flaws and ways in which they are very human and unique:

Best characteristic:s, strengths, what people generally think of them

Name: _____   Date: _____

My Character

History

I was able to spend a weekend at the Anne Frank House at their education center with teachers from all over Europe. It was pretty amazing. I feel really fortunate to have experienced this. I discovered while I was there that they have a bookstore with tons of publications, all in different languages, and they sell online (https://webshop.annefrank.org/en/books). I picked up copies of Anne's diary in French and Italian—languages I was working on during my visit.

Providing learners with a topic about which they have some knowledge is an effective way to build language skills.

Magazines

Magazines are high-interest because they are niche and therefore easy to connect learners to texts. They also have great visuals. While it isn't possible for most of us to have access to an infinite stream of current print TL magazines, we can access this type of content online. Many libraries have apps to help with this.

Audiobooks

I love audiobooks. I'm a really busy person, and they allow me to still consume great content. I can listen while I clean, commute, or walk.

Not only do beginning language courses have lots of content for some of the big novels that are translated into many languages, but they carry content from other cultures as well.

For advanced classes, consider listening to a book together. It might be one chapter at a time. Allow them to follow along with the text.

AI is making high-interest audio available for reading alongside. Many browsers now have a function that will read text to learners and have built-in tools to look up unknown words.

Reading Journals

Keep journals of facts from your reading. They make reading active. Consider these reading journal activities:

1. Write ten facts from the chapter you read.
2. Write interesting quotes.
3. Recap what you read.
4. Retell the story.
5. Write a review.
6. Write a letter to the author or one of the characters/people in the piece.

Uncomfortable Conversations

Tim Ferriss once said that "A person's success in life can be measured by the number of uncomfortable conversations he or she is willing to have."

I think it's relevant to language learning because all of your conversations are going to be uncomfortable up to a certain point. It can be quite demoralizing and uncomfortable to get through it. Right?

If you have more of those conversations, you're going to get better at languages. Eventually, they won't be uncomfortable anymore.

Ferriss described learning to read in Japanese and building his skills. He said that in high school he had a "nasty manga habit." He would stay up and read, doing his pleasure in reading another language.

Going back to those hyperpolyglots: this is a way to do it. You don't need anybody to talk to you. You don't need to be in the target language country. You just need to get your hands on some materials.

That Oprah's Book Club feeling is the best in the world for many. Feeling really immersed and fully engaged in a good book with your feet up, sipping a cup of coffee (or drink of your choice), can be the perfect escape. To do that and to be able to learn new languages at the same time—that's the ultimate. Invest time and effort in reading high-interest content.

More Tools to Make Text Comprehensible

Use these organizers to dig deep into the text, mining and acquiring much language in context along the way.

Reading ◆ 115

What Happened in the Story?

What happened in the story?

Title of the Story:

First,

Next,

Last,

Name: _____ Date: _____

What Happened in the Story?

5 W's Book Summary

- Name:
- Date:
- What happened?
- When did it happen?
- Where did it happen?
- Who was involved?
- Why did it happen?

5 W's Book Summary

The Hand Reading Summary

The Hand Reading Summary

Readlang Browser Extension

Sign up for this clever browser extension—https://readlang.com. It will help you read and curate interesting content in your target language. Their tools make reading comprehensible.

Reference

Krashen, Stephen.2017) "Polyglots and the Comprehension Hypothesis." *Turkish Online Journal of English Language Teaching*, vol. 2, no. 3, 2017: pp. 113–119. https://sdkrashen.com/content/articles/2017_polyglots_.pdf. Accessed 28 July 2023.

7

Pair Work and Speaking

Getting students talking in the target language is the core of the language teacher's job. In this chapter, we'll explore some activities to get the conversations going.

Bloom's taxonomy works beautifully with our language standards and desired outcomes. We have to walk before we can run. In terms of language proficiency, we need to provide students with structured activities and support until they can be more self-directed. We work at the lower levels until they build the skills to do work at the higher levels.

We want engagement, not just compliance from our students. These activities can be done at both the Novice/A and Intermediate/B range. The length, complexity of the task, and output will be different according to proficiency range. Once learners have enough words and phrases, they can create with language and have entered the Intermediate/B range. Bottom line: shorter for Novice/A, longer for Intermediate/B. Novice/A— words, phrases moving into the sentence level. Intermediate/B— phrases, sentences moving into the paragraph level.

Research-Based Interviews

Interviews are invaluable because they can practice several modes of communication, providing students opportunities to read, write, speak, listen, and engage in culture.

DOI: 10.4324/9781032622507-12

#1: Connect this to a student research project. A way to do this is to research singers and celebrities in the target language. The students then write the questions and can send them to the subject. Their reps often respond (even if it isn't personal), and they will have had that interaction. Sometimes they do respond themselves (how exciting!).

#2: Research and play the part of the celebrity.

Getting some movement and interaction can make an activity that might have a lot of repetition (essential for retention of learning and acquisition) feel fresh and new. Consider having the students stand in two lines or two circles, create one large circle or allow students to speak to each other in a less-structured way. Have them interview the person across from them, speak in pairs or groups (similar to real life), or do this a large group to add more listening for all.

Use music as a way to provide cultural input. Stopping it is the signal to change speaking partners. Each time the music changes, talk to someone new, or play music in the background as students interview each other.

Break out as a whole class with all of the questions after students have had lots of practice. This can also be a great class pen-pal activity, where the questions are asked via letters.

More Activities with Questions and Answers

Questions and answers are a highly effective way to practice real communication. Learners practice pronunciation, reduce anxiety, learn grammar and vocabulary in context, and build listening skills all through this simple structure. This activity can also easily be modified to any level or communicative theme. Using questions and answers to learn and acquire language is supported by research and can be a fast track to fluency.

#1: Structured Input

I recommend offering learners opportunities to practice and answer via structured input. They can also create questions and answers. This is appropriate, of course, but will take more time.

Here is an example of asking and answering questions about last weekend in French. There is an accompanying presentation with visuals. It is vital for learners to get a lot of input. This activity can be done often, building competency in their narration skills in the context of their real life.

Tu as fait du shopping?
Oui, j'ai fait du shopping.
Ou: Non, je n'ai pas fait de shopping.
Tu es resté(e) à la maison?
Oui, je suis resté(e) à la maison.
Ou: Non, je ne suis pas resté(e) à lamaison.
Tu as réussi à faire quelque chose d'amusant?
Oui, j'ai réussi à faire quelque chose d'amusant.
Ou: Non, je n'ai pas réussi à faire quoi que ce soit d'amusant.
Tu es allé(e) au cinéma?
Oui, je suis allé(e) au cinéma.
Ou: Non, je ne suis pas allé(e) au cinéma.
Tu as regardé un film?
Oui, j'ai regardé un film.
Ou: Non, je n'ai pas regardé de film.
Tu as eu à étudier?
Oui, j'ai eu à étudier.
Ou: Non je n'ai pas eu à étudier.
Tu as fait ton devoir?
Oui, j'ai fait mon devoir.
Ou: Non, je n'ai pas fait mon devoir.
Tu as étudié?
Oui, j'ai étudié.
Ou: Non, je n'ai pas étudié.
Tu es allé(e) à la bibliothèque?
Oui, je suis allé(e) à la bibliothèque.
Ou: Non, je ne suis pas allé(e) à la bibliothèque.
Tu es allé(e) au restaurant?
Oui, je suis allé(e) au restaurant.
Ou: Non, je ne suis pas allé(e) au restaurant.
Tu as joué aux jeux vidéo?
Oui, j'ai joué aux jeux vidéo.
Ou: Non, je n'ai pas joué aux jeux vidéo.

Tu as eu à travailler?
Oui, j'ai eu à travailler.
Ou: Non, je n'ai pas eu à travailler.
Tu as eu à faire le ménage?
Oui, j'ai eu à faire le ménage.
Ou: Non, je n'ai pas eu à faire le ménage.
Tu as fait ton lit?
Oui, j'ai fait mon lit.
Ou: Non, je n'ai pas fait mon lit.
Tu as fait les courses?
Oui, j'ai fait les courses.
Ou: Non, je n'ai pas fait les courses.

#2: Fake Glasses

I've found a fun tool to do question-and-answer activities: fake glasses. Students can write on the "glasses" with dry erase markers. Students write questions. They then travel around the room and use them to talk to classmates.

#3: Questions Sheet/Chart/Clipboard

Students prepare questions, interact, and take notes. Debrief as a class or extend it into a writing activity. This serves as an effective way to practice structures in the third person.

Here's a simple chart that will work with any communicative theme:

Table 7.1

Questions	Answers

Notes:

Organize questions and answers in this chart. Adjust the size of the rows and columns to correspond with the number of speakers and/or questions and answers.

#4: Interviews based on cultural research

One person plays the role of someone, and the other person asks them questions. It's an effective way to practice speaking: to take these characters from your TL culture that are in these dialogues and then expand them. The students are taking on the persona and adding details to what they do.

Consider having the questions and answers recorded. Rhinospike is great for this. The students can hear their lines read by a native speaker as they're being learned. Actors do this all the time. They listen to recordings of nuances of speech to accurately portray a character's accent and speech patterns. Of course, you're the director, and your job is to give notes to help them improve. It's a really powerful language lesson.

#5: Cháchara Circular

This fabulous variation of Q & A chat was shared with me by Spanish teacher Andrea Nazelli. It can be adapted to any language, level, and theme. Students shouldn't use questions that can be answered just yes or no, or with one word.

- ◆ Hand out the sheet.
- ◆ Give students time to create questions based on your topic and set a goal for speaking.
- ◆ Students should sit in a circle or rectangle/square. Consider two circles/rectangles for larger groups or doing it on separate days.
- ◆ Students talk. Students use their sheet for support, taking notes about their classmates' answers and tallying the number of times they participate. Provide them with support as needed.
- ◆ Students finish with self-reflection.

Cháchara Circular is student-centered and student-led, and can be used both formatively and summatively. Andrea says this works beautifully with unit tests and speaking portions of final exams, and suggests combining student self-reflections with assessment criteria that you have selected.

Table 7.2 Cháchara Circular: Structured Activity for Conversation for Novice/A-Range

Nombre: _____
Fecha: _____ **Hora:** _____
TEMA(S): _____

Hoy, quiero hablar _____ **veces.** ¿Has realizado tu meta hoy?

Sí _____ *todavía no* _____

Mis preguntas:

1.
2.
3.
4.
5.

5	4	3	2	1	pronunciación	___ Usé una variedad de vocabulario
5	4	3	2	1	iniciativo	___ No usé inglés.
5	4	3	2	1	vocabulario	___ Realicé mi meta.
5	4	3	2	1	gramática	___ Invité a otros a participar.
5	4	3	2	1	entusiasmo	___ Usé frases completas.
5	4	3	2	1	participación	___ Esperé mi turno.
						___ Hablé del tema.
						___ Escuché bien.

Mi total: total: NOTAL FINAL:

_____   +   _____   =   _____

Guest Speakers and Special Person Interviews

#1: Guest Speakers

Guest speakers can provide a change of pace and a variety of essential input.

Some are lucky enough to have contacts come to your class and chat with students. This provides invaluable practice and exposure to a variety of speakers.

Getting students talking to native speakers builds proficiency fast. Learners practice learned language and acquire through the responses they hear.

This activity was created from my experience as an independent language learner and can get those speakers into your room if they are otherwise unavailable. It is designed to get you understanding and speaking new languages fast by providing practice and listening comprehension practice. There are supports built in for Novice and Intermediate learners.

Prepare your questions. Before the interview, the students should prepare by researching and writing questions. Focus on some cultural questions specific to the speaker's country after getting a bit of biographical information.

Use Google Docs (or any other way that is collaborative) to do this part of the project. There is a lot of accountability in doing this collaboratively and making the preparation part of the grade. The Google Doc also allows for great collaboration from anywhere.

Edit the document. Students can be responsible for creating their own questions, doing research, and correcting/editing one another's content before the lesson. You will get to see all of their work before they actually conduct the interview. You can focus on accuracy and not duplicating questions this way as well.

Practice. Practice a few times with the tech side of things. This will look different, of course, depending on what you use. Record the session and use it as a listening exercise or with students who were absent.

Do the interview. Students will hate this at first, but it is a great way to introduce them in a supervised way to native speakers they wouldn't normally interact with. The questions really do help here, and they will be grateful that they prepared ahead of time.

Students should note the answers in the document during the interview. They will likely need to speak to other students to confirm some answers. Allow this, as it requires more communicative practice in the target language.

Seriously consider recording the interview. This can serve as an engaging activity for years.

Summarize. Students should write a summary of the interview in the target language. Let them select a certain number of details to report back to you. It is a good way to get them to review their notes and synthesize the language and content they used.

Hire an online tutor for the students to interview.

The first step is setting up an account at italki or another online language tutoring platform.

There are teachers from all over the world teaching many languages. They will ask you a few questions about your goals, native language, etc. After answering the questions and confirming my email, I was able to start searching for a teacher. The teacher profiles have ratings, information on rates, and testimonials.

There will be a section on the teacher's page where they will talk about how they deliver lessons. They can give lessons via FaceTime, Google Meet, Zoom, Skype, or Google Hangouts.

They have many filters to help you find exactly what you need with regard to schedule, communication tool, price, country, etc.

Ready to do this? The first time might be difficult, but I think you'll love it. It is a great way to get your students interacting with natives from your target language, build their confidence while they build their communicative skills, and become more proficient with some great tools out there to learn any language they wish.

#2 Special Person Interview

Find a native or proficient speaker of the target language who is willing to participate in the interview. This person could be a community member, a parent, a teacher, or someone connected to the school.

Before the interview, prepare a set of questions. Encourage students to create a mix of general and specific questions about topics such as family, traditions, hobbies, career, and cultural

126 ◆ Pair Work and Speaking

practices. Ensure that the questions align with the language proficiency level of your students.

Students take notes during the interview to aid in their understanding and future discussions.

Assign one or two students as interviewers. They will lead the interview by asking the prepared questions while the rest of the class observes and takes notes. After the initial set of questions, open the floor to the rest of the class for follow-up questions. This allows students to go deeper into specific topics or areas of interest that may arise during the interview.

Amy Marshall at Zona de Profes conducts her special person interviews for learners and not guests. Essentially, all students take a turn being the interviewee. They are to be able to respond to certain topics. She provides them with amazing support through comprehensible input via digital word walls. I was lucky enough to get to see her share how she conducts these. Her tip on getting a digital pointer for even more support during the interviews is priceless.

Some words from Amy on these:

> Special person interviews are one way to build a tight-knit and supportive community in your classroom while using the target language. The teacher will have a volunteer come to the front of the class to sit for an interview that is led by the teacher, who provides language support such as question words, high-frequency verbs, and vocabulary related to the line of questioning that the student can refer to during the interview. As the interview progresses, the teacher gathers basic biographical information (name, where they are from/live, how old they are, and birthdate, as well as a description of personality attributes), and then allows the student to choose one from a variety of topics (family, pets, activities, fears, childhood, future plans, etc.) that they would like to answer more questions about. This keeps the

interviews interesting, as the students choose what they want to talk about, and different topics will be discussed with different students. The teacher will ask a question of the student (first and second person) and then report to the class what she has learned about the student (third person). The teacher will then confirm with the student by re-asking the question (either in a slightly different way or with incorrect information), allowing the student to repeat the correct information. The teacher will then ask questions of the class to confirm that they have understood the information given.

The teacher can ask yes or no questions or use a question word to elicit the information from the class. If the student shares a piece of information that seems compelling, the teacher stops and spends time talking about it. More questions are asked, and more details are gathered.

Spend time enjoying what everyone in the class enjoys and find commonalities between other members of the class by asking the class as a whole questions. An interview can go for 10 to 15 minutes depending on the comfort level of the student and the interest of the class. Once finished, take the time to create a text with your class about what you have learned about the interviewed student by asking guiding questions of the class to recreate the interview in paragraph form. You can write this on the board or type it and project it on the screen. Students will copy this down into their notebooks. Eventually, each student will have a page about each other student in their notebook. The student who was interviewed will write their version in the first person and the other students will write in the third person. These texts can be used for comparison and contrast as well as games and writing activities.

TL Support for Special Person Interviews

Language Experience Approach

If you are unfamiliar with this, it may just only be in nomenclature. Essentially, you build out written and spoken language with students. This might be building a survey in front of them as you deliver the questions in comprehensible input. Write down what they say, providing more visual prompts for further speech. All of these activities can be initially built this way and redone for years.

Surveys

#1: This can be done in class using tables and be reused for years.

Table 7.3 Sample survey to talk about favorite activities

¿Cuál es tu actividad favorita?	
actividad	nombre de persona
jugar a los videojuegos	
nadar	
leer	

pasar tiempo con los amigos	
ver la tele	
cocinar	
escuchar música	
jugar deportes	
estudiar	
ir de compras	

Here's a blank table to fill in with what you'd like. Some ideas:

- foods they like
- family members
- places they'd like to travel
- classes
- hair and eye color
- favorite colors
- favorite activities
- favorite sports.

Table 7.4 Blank Template to Create Surveys on Any Topic

#2: The electronic form version allows students to take a survey online. You can then use the results as visual speaking prompts.

130 ◆ Pair Work and Speaking

Likes and dislikes, or anything where students might provide a preference or an opinion, can be done using a simple table drawn on a board with the headings being their choices. They might place Post-its in the category of their choice. A student can even serve as scribe and write their name. A Jamboard works nicely, too. Use what was created as a speaking prompt.

Show and Tell

This classic activity from kindergarten is a gem for language classes. Students bring in something and share it with the class in the target language. I suggest theming it (e.g., an important photo, a toy you loved).

Did You Do It?

This activity is a variation of *Have you ever?* and is appropriate for the end of the first or second year. It is designed specifically to practice simple past tenses. It can also be done in upper levels with more complex prompts.

Everyone comes together in a circle and puts up their fingers (you choose the number).

Each student will have prepared a certain number of questions that can be answered with yes or no, and people will put their fingers down as they're being eliminated. For example: *Did you eat bread today?* No, I didn't, so I put my finger down. *Did you walk to school today?* No. *Did you watch a movie last week?* Use anything that can be answered with yes or no. It's a great way to recycle any type of introductory personal information.

This can be done with some kind of token as well. Students deposit tokens somewhere (a bag, a container of some kind). Making the tokens culturally relevant is a plus. Create a language experience activity by summarizing the results on the board with students.

Transform Textbook Activities into Pair Work

Any activity in your text can be made communicative and interactive. Some simple ideas to do so:

- Complete with a partner.
- Sit in two lines or small groups and work through the exercise with the person across from you.
- Look at the real-life task the exercise is intended to fulfill. Are they being asked to do descriptions? Narration? A journal entry? Make it a short dramatization or recording instead.

Chat Mats

Chat mats are an effective way to get people talking. Think visuals or chunks.

Students are given a task. In this case, it is to draw a person and write some simple sentences to describe their person. Next, they work with a partner to describe their person. Their partner should draw what they hear. Next, students change roles.

The following step is to compare what was drawn to the original. The last step is to describe the other person's drawing in writing. Finally, create a gallery.

Chat mats can be created once and used over and over. Some ideas:

- Last weekend (take my French version and adapt).
- Last vacation (see my Spanish version below).
- Classes. Using a table, students fill in their schedules. Provide some questions if needed. Get them talking. I share my chart below.
- Homes. Have a floor plan. Students give clues to their partner about the room they are thinking of, and their partner guesses. An idea might be to use one of the dream house projects done with much detail and clarity

132 ◆ Pair Work and Speaking

a student made and reproduce it with their permission. Laminate it, and then you have a chat mat to speak about rooms and furniture.

◆ Any theme can be illustrated quickly by students. They sketch according to your parameters. This is an effective TPR listening activity, too.

¿Qué hiciste durante las últimas vacaciones?
"What did you do last weekend?"
Remember to answer with the yo form of the preterit.
¿Viajaste durante las últimas vacaciones? Sí, yo viajé. O No, no viajé.
¿Comiste comida buena?
Sí, comí comida buena. O No, no comí comida buena.
¿Estudiaste durante las últimas vacaciones? Sí, estudié. O No, no estudié.
¿Escuchaste música durante las últimas vacaciones? Sí, escuché. O No, no escuché.
¿Bailaste durante las últimas vacaciones? Sí, bailé. O No, no bailé.
¿Visitaste con tu familia durante las últimas vacaciones? Sí, visité con mi familia. O No, no visité con mi familia.
¿Cocinaste durante las últimas vacaciones? Sí, cociné. O No, no cociné.
¿Leíste un libro durante las últimas vacaciones? Sí, leí un libro. O No, no leí un libro.

Time	Mon	Tue	Wed	Thu	Fri
07:00 am					
08:00 am					
09:00 am					
10:00 am					
11:00 am					
12:00 pm					
01:00 pm					
02:00 pm					
03:00 pm					
04:00 pm					
05:00 pm					
06:00 pm					

Class Schedules

Have students write out their schedules. Have them use these to ask other students about their schedules.

Descriptions

Step #1. Read the phrases on the cheat sheet.
Step #2. Write a description of a person using at least ten traits. This person can be real or imaginary.
Step #3. Describe this person to a classmate. They should draw what you say. Do not use English or look at their drawings.
Step #4. Verify their drawing based on your original sentences.

Step #5. Switch roles and repeat.
Step #6. Write your own description of the person you drew. Name them.
Step #7. Create a gallery of the masterpieces!

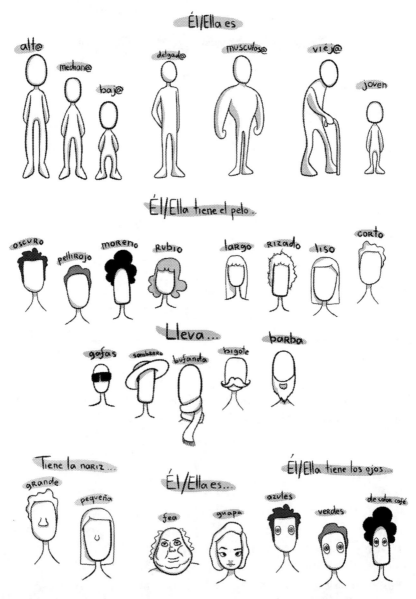

Descriptions Chat Mat

Use words and phrases on the chat mat to describe people.

Presentations/Speaking Activities

I think that this word "presentations" is often daunting. You'll hear it throughout this book because presentations are essential for building skills. They can be done in small groups, one on one, and can be short and simple.

One suggestion for graded pair work and presentations is to let people practice in small groups/pairs. You then move around the room. If students need more time, they can have it. It is far less intimidating, as they aren't in front of the whole class.

Try to work in a visual whenever you can for support. Graphic organizers work beautifully for this (find several in the online Appendices). Storyboards really help, too (again, a blank one is included for you). They can use this to create a comic strip to practice narration by drawing the photos and adding captions. Anything that provides the support they need works. For example, a paper plate with foods drawn on it to help students talk about what they like to eat. Students might bring in a toy or other item for show and tell. A simple slide to add bullet points or a photo can serve as great help to students' confidence to speak.

Sometimes more formal presentations are appropriate. These are especially important to help students learn more about the TL cultures. I recommend keeping them simple. They might make a slide show and share a few things that allow students to produce the target language at their proficiency level. The slides can serve as support. Make it interactive by handing out Post-it notes and having students write feedback in the target language (review beforehand for Novice/A learners) or write questions for the presenter. Everyone places their Post-its on a piece of paper for the presenter to read their feedback.

Dice

Dice are fun and tactile and can provide a game-like feeling to an activity. Consider this fun template for prompts below:

Table 7.5 Dice

	1	2	3	4	5	6
1	question /topic	question /topic	question /topic	question /topic	question /topic	question /topic
2	question /topic	question /topic	question /topic	question /topic	question /topic	question /topic
3	question /topic	question /topic	question /topic	question /topic	question /topic	question /topic
4	question /topic	question /topic	question /topic	question /topic	question /topic	question /topic
5	question /topic	question /topic	question /topic	question /topic	question /topic	question /topic
6	question /topic	question /topic	question /topic	question /topic	question /topic	question /topic

Use the prompts with dice for conversation starters.

M.A.S.H.

"M.A.S.H." is a paper-and-pencil fortune-telling game. Basically, categories are filled in to decide the player's fortunes. Living arrangements (mansion, apartment, shack, or house), names of potential partners, desired locations, number and gender of kids, types of cars, jobs, and pets are common categories, but adapt this to fit your curricular objectives and themes.

A spiral is drawn in the center box, and the fortune teller stops when the person getting their fortune says "stop." The number of lines in the spiral determines the magic number.

Let's say the magic number is four. Starting from the beginning, every fourth item is crossed out until only one remains in each category. The fortune teller fills in the results and reads the fortune based on the remaining choices in each category.

Pair Work and Speaking ◆ 137

Table 7.6 M.A.S.H. Template

M.A.S.H.
(mansion, apartment, shack, house)

Future Category #1	Future Category #2
1. _____	1. _____
2. _____	2. _____
3. _____	3. _____
4. _____	4. _____
Future Category #3	Future Category #4
1. _____	1. _____
2. _____	2. _____
3. _____	3. _____
4. _____	4. _____

Spiral Box

Magic # _____

Change the template to the categories/themes you are exploring.

Review Project

Many language programs have this simple activity at some point. Essentially, students create a short autobiography, so this likely won't be new to you.

This activity is a simple set of questions derived from content that reviews the previous level and covers a lot of themes. You can include any you want from your previous course. Some obvious

138 ◆ Pair Work and Speaking

ones would be simple autobiographical information such as name, place of birth, date of birth, and interests and hobbies. Then you can infuse and include more activities from your course (e.g., foods, what your house looks like, what you do in your spare time).

Here is an example in French:

1. Comment tu t'appelles? // What's your name?
   Je m'appelle... // My name is...

2. Tu vis où? // Where do you live?
   Je vis à... // I live in...

3. Tu viens d'où? // Where are you from?
   Je viens de... // I am from...

4. Tu as quel âge? // How old are you?5.
   J'ai __ ans. // I am __ years old.

5. C'est quand ton anniversaire? // When is your birthday?
   Mon anniversaire est le __ ____. // My birthday is the __ of ____.
       janvier
       février
       mars
       avril
       mai
       juin
       juillet
       août
       septembre
       octobre
       novembre
       décembre

6. Tu es né où? // Where were you born?
   Je suis né à ____. // I was born in ____.

Pair Work and Speaking ◆ 139

7. Parle-nous de ta famille. // Tell us about your family.
   Ma famille est... // My family is...
   grande
   petite

8. Tu as des frères et sœurs? Combien? Comment ils s'appellent? // Do you have siblings? How many? What are their names?
   J'ai __ frères et sœurs. // I have __ siblings.

9. Décris ta personnalité et ton aspect physique. Tu es comment? Écris un minimum de cinq phrases. // Describe your personality and appearance. What do you look like? Write a minimum of five sentences. Je suis... // I am...
   aimable
   sympathique
   intelligent(e)
   sportif/sportive
   fort(e)
   organisé/organisée
   studieux/studieuse
   travailleur/travailleuse
   grand(e)
   de taille moyenne
   blond(e)
   brun(e)
   châtain

10. Tu as quelles matières? Combien? Quand? // What classes do you have? How many? When?
    J'ai... // I have...
    anglais
    espagnol
    français
    mathématiques

sciences
art
musique
algèbre
géométrie
calcul
histoire
technologie
éducation physique

11. Tu as fait quoi durant l'été dernier? // What did you do last summer?
J'ai (Je n'ai pas) voyagé
J'ai (Je n'ai pas) étudié
J'ai (Je n'ai pas) travaillé
J'ai (Je n'ai pas) fait du sport
J'ai (Je n'ai pas) dessiné
J'ai (Je n'ai pas) fait la cuisine
J'ai (Je n'ai pas) lu
J'ai (Je n'ai pas) regardé la télévision

12. Tu parles quelles langues? // What languages do you speak?
Je parle... // I speak...
anglais
espagnol
arabe
japonais
chinois
français
italien

13. Décris ta routine quotidienne. // Describe your daily routine.
Je me réveille à... // I wake up at...
Je me lève à... // I get up at...

Je prends une douche. // I take a shower.
Je me maquille. // I put on makeup.
Je m'habille. // I get dressed.Je me brosse les
dents. // I brush my teeth.Je sors. // I leave.
Je travaille. // I work.
Je vais à mes cours. // I go to my classes.
Je déjeune. // I eat lunch.
Je rentre à la maison. // I go home.

14. Où aimes-tu aller faire du shopping? // Where do
you like to go shopping?
J'aime aller à ____. // I like to go to ____.

15. Tu pratiques un sport? // Do you play sports?
Je joue au... // I play...
tennis
golf
volleyball
football
football Américain
baseball

16. Quel est ton film préféré? // What is your favorite
movie?
Mon film préféré est ____. // My favorite movie is
____.

17. Quel est ton repas préféré? // What is your favorite
food?
Mon repas préféré est ____. // My favorite food is
____.

18. Quelle est ton émission de télévision préférée? //
What is your favorite television show?
Mon émission préférée est ____. // My favorite
show is ____.

142 ◆ Pair Work and Speaking

Give students choices to complete this task. It might be an essay, a presentation, a video, an audio recording, a photo with text overlay, or a book. Another way to approach this is to get a large sheet of butcher paper. Have students draw an outline of themselves. They can label their body parts and answer the questions on their paper. You will be impressed with what they create.

Slides

Visual prompts serve as useful input to stimulate speaking. Consider this activity on daily routines. Start by talking about your routine and write in on the board. Show students a slide of another person and their routine. Next, have students rewrite your routine in the third person.

La rutina diaria—https://docs.google.com/presentation/d/1cNjguqJ_1FdqDAf-8-ztXNp7NSLvppzg1cryDNFBlbM/edit#slide=id.g11235168402_0_0

The next example is a presentation of travel tasks. The slides serve as stimuli for dialogues.

www.canva.com/design/DAFeePxpQnE/CPow150Ru4Ii0h08WED8mw/edit?utm_content=DAFeePxpQnE&utm_campaign=designshare&utm_medium=link2&utm_source=sharebutton

Students should play the roles depicted in the slides. They can write lines, practice and present the scenario. The last example serves as an effective starter for a Novice class. Essentially, it is a slide with speech bubbles asking basic questions such as who, where, when, and what is happening. Use often to reinforce the skill of making questions, or as a warm up.

Get your copy in the digital resources.
www.canva.com/design/DAFeZaEtVIM/B_VkNv7odjrcQR0wB5yxKg/edit?utm_content=DAFeZaEtVIM&utm_campaign=designshare&utm_medium=link2&utm_source=sharebutton

Recordings

This is another activity to do once you've established an atmosphere where people are comfortable taking risks in the target language.

Recordings can be intimidating. People often say they hate the sound of their voice or don't like how they look on video (I can relate). However, it's probably one of the best decisions a language learner or a teacher can make to start recording regularly for numerous reasons. A lot of assessments require us to record. However, even if that's not something you have to prepare the students for, it's still a great activity.

Regular recordings serve as a fantastic documentation of progress. For these beginning-level classes, it couldn't be more valuable. Once you get over the first couple of uncomfortable times of recording due to students not wanting to do it, shyness, technical difficulties, or anything else you can imagine, students will be willing to do this.

#1: Recording Dialogues

Most textbooks have dialogues at the beginning levels. They're an excellent way to get students using survival language and to review. Have students rehearse and record these.

#2: Recording Conversations

Have students bullet-point out some things they want to talk about and have them record these. The recordings can be as short as two or three minutes. They can be sort of painful to get through the process the first couple of times due to technical difficulties, students not wanting to record, or students not really understanding what to do. Once they get comfortable with sitting down and talking, they'll be fine with it. These recordings will serve as a great documentation of progress.

Students might record a project or assignment in lieu of writing it (a great way to give them choices). Another way is to just simply record, saying whatever comes to mind (I love this as a learner).

144 ◆ Pair Work and Speaking

Have students record in groups, pairs, or talking to themselves. It's a great way to get over shyness in a foreign language.

Scavenger/Treasure Hunt

Scavenger/treasure hunts are so useful because they get students speaking, and they also make for great community builders for your beginning-level classes. A beginning-level class might take a few minutes in groups with a list of essentials in your classroom to find. Remember when we labeled those items in the classroom? You can give students a list of those. They must go around and find them while collecting some kind of documentation.

Some items to consider:

- ◆ labeled items in your target language
- ◆ survival language
- ◆ your reading library.

These hunts also make for great cultural explorations. Students might search for places in the TL country. This might be art, stores, or places of interest.

Scavenger hunts are best done with a strong and clear purpose. Authenticity is always best. They might find 20 dishes from the TL country. As a class, go through them, planning which you can actually make and try in class. You might provide them with a list of experiences one might have visiting the TL country (i.e., experiencing Christmas in France or visiting the flea markets in Paris). They should research them, provide a short description, and share which one they'd most like to have.

Guess Who?

Learners use the target language to learn basic descriptions in a beginning world language class. Have a cheat sheet card to help students play the game completely in the target language.

Devine qui?

Guess Who? Card

More advanced students have to be able to play the game completely in the target language without the use of the card. They also need to be able to describe the members in the game and all the faces and characters they see.

Visual Cheat Sheet to Help Students Play the Classic Game *Guess Who?*

Find an editable cheat sheet in the resources.

To do this as a group, an individual selects a classmate. Classmates ask those closed questions until they guess who the mystery person is.

146 ◆ Pair Work and Speaking

Guessing games are a ton of fun and easy to create. Some topics:

- clothing
- descriptions
- likes and dislikes
- hair color.

Describe class members or people you know. Students guess who is being described.

Debate

Debates can be done when students hit the Intermediate/B-range and can create with language.

First, select a topic. The best are related to your theme and topic, high-interest yet neutral enough to not cause serious disputes, and for which students can find supporting sources in the target language. Some ideas:

- public transportation v. cars
- social media: harmful or helpful?
- life in the city or countryside
- audiobooks or traditional books
- culture or adventure travel.

These are also best done in teams at this language proficiency level. Teams can research, develop arguments together, and practice leading up to the debate.

Here's a basic framework:

- Introduction: Provide a brief introduction to the topic and explain its relevance.
- Opening statements: The first speaker presents their argument and key points.
- Rebuttal: The second speaker presents their counterargument and disputes the first speaker's points.
- Cross-examination: Both speakers ask and answer questions to clarify and challenge each other's arguments.

Pair Work and Speaking ◆ 147

- ◆ Final statements: Both speakers provide their final thoughts and summarize their main points.
- ◆ Conclusion: Summarize the key points and end the debate.

Assign specific time periods for each section of the debate based on your numbers, time available, and size of the teams.

Speed Dating

Speed dating simulations are so useful because you can incorporate so many modes of communication. They're interactive and engaging.

Add an element of culture by having students take on the persona of someone from your TL culture. I suggest writing down specific places on slips of paper and allowing students to choose. They can trade if they wish or suggest another place.

Provide a set of questions for them to research their character (basic biographical information is necessary), as well as some further questions. Some ideas:

- ◆ What is your favorite book/movie/TV show and why?
- ◆ If you could travel anywhere in the world, where would you go and why?
- ◆ What do you enjoy doing in your free time?
- ◆ What is your favorite type of cuisine?
- ◆ Do you have any pets? Tell me about them!
- ◆ What's the most adventurous thing you've ever done?
- ◆ What are your career goals or aspirations?
- ◆ Are you more of an introvert or an extrovert?
- ◆ What is something you're passionate about?
- ◆ Do you have any hidden talents?

Set the desks up in pairs. Have students make name tags. Provide students with a sheet to take notes about the people they "met."

148 ◆ Pair Work and Speaking

Speed Dating Template

Name: _____

Age: _____

Interests/Hobbies: _____

Name: _____

Age: _____

Interests/Hobbies: _____

Name: _____

Age: _____

Interests/Hobbies: _____

Name: _____

Age: _____

Interests/Hobbies: _____

Name: _____

Age: _____

Interests/Hobbies: _____

Name: _____

Age: _____

Interests/Hobbies: _____

Name: _____

Age: _____

Interests/Hobbies: _____

Change to your target language for student characters to "meet" for the first time.

Chat in Class

When I was a child, I asked my Uncle Benner how he learned Spanish. Benner is a Harvard-educated attorney (both law and undergraduate) who practiced international, corporate, and intellectual property law in the U.S. and Venezuela. Benner is a person of sharp intellect and outstanding character. He credits his entrance and success at Harvard to being provided with the opportunity and privilege by my grandparents and firmly believes he is not special. Despite receiving a top-notch formal education, his response was that the best way to learn Spanish is to get a beer, sit down, and talk to people.

That is clearly not an option for so many reasons, but the idea resonates with me to this day.

Sitting around for a visit with something to drink and snack on, feeling comfortable and relaxed, is one of the best ways to practice language skills. The idea is backed by research as well. With a lower affective filter, we are more willing to take the necessary risks to communicate in new languages.

Variation #1: Chat

Advanced classes can easily make the conversation flow, but less-skilled speakers can also practice, too. Let students bullet-point topics out. They can also be provided with a sheet of topics. See the example below:

- Hi, how are you doing?
- What's your name?
- Can you introduce yourself?
- Where are you from?
- Do you speak (target language)?
- Tell us about what you are wearing.
- Tell us what is in your backpack.
- What language do you want to learn?
- What's your favorite food?
- What do you like to do for fun?
- What's your favorite TV show or movie?
- Have you visited any other countries?
- What's something interesting about your culture?
- Do you have any hobbies?
- What's your favorite type of music?
- Can you teach me a new word or phrase in this language?

150 ◆ Pair Work and Speaking

- ◆ Tell us about your house.
- ◆ List your classes.
- ◆ Tell us about your family.
- ◆ Tell us about yourself.

Give learners some time to collaborate and make notes before they start. Join a table and speak. Switch to a new group when you hear a signal from the teacher. Recycle your question/chat cards from previous units.

#2: At the Table

A variation of this is At the Table. Bring in (or make in class with an authentic recipe) TL food and drink (even simple drinks like hot chocolate will do) and have a chat.

#3: Gratitude/Question Jar

Infuse gratitude into your language classes. It's an important life lesson. It also provides some great context within which to teach languages.

One of my very favorite activities is gratitude journals. I discovered these during a difficult period of my life. I wrote down every day no fewer than 25 things to be grateful for. It can be really hard, especially when you're feeling down. However, it forces you to search for the good things, no matter how small they might be. For example, a sunny day or a cup of peppermint tea.

These are great in language class, too. Have students do a similar activity. Do them in much shorter tasks. For example, share five things you're grateful for or ten things you're grateful for.

Some ideas:

- ◆ People you are grateful for
- ◆ A color you love
- ◆ A favorite activity
- ◆ A great day you'll have in the future
- ◆ Things that are nice to look at

Recycle question slips. Cut into strips and keep in a jar for these chat activities.

More Activities with Cards

While you can have students use the cards they create for activities such as Charades or Pictionary, you can also have them write out situations/tasks.

#1: Review Role Plays

Write out situations on cards, or take from your unit's communicative task goals. The most efficient way to do this is to go through the communicative tasks of your unit. For example, they might learn to order a drink at a coffee shop or meet someone new for the first time. More advanced tasks might be complaining at a restaurant.

#2: Conversation Cards

Remember those routines we talked about? Here are some examples of questions created from reviewing a beginning course. Learners do Q and A in groups using the cards.

At the first stage, they can take some time to read through, understand the questions, and craft their responses.

1. What is your name?
2. Where are you from?
3. How old are you?
4. What is your favorite color?
5. Do you have any siblings? How many?
6. What is your favorite food?
7. What is your favorite hobby?
8. Do you like to read? What kind of books do you like?
9. Do you have any pets? What are their names?
10. What is your favorite sport?

152 ◆ Pair Work and Speaking

11. Can you describe your best friend?
12. What is your favorite subject in school?
13. What do you want to be when you grow up?
14. Do you like to sing or dance? Can you show us a little?
15. What is your favorite season?
16. Can you tell us about your last vacation?
17. What is your favorite animal? Why?
18. What is your favorite movie or TV show?
19. Do you play any musical instruments?
20. Can you teach us a few words or phrases in (target language)?

An engaging way to get lots of practice and lots of talking is to divide students into groups according to your classroom geography. For example, you may have students in six or seven different groups. Assign students a number and have them practice with that group. After they have had some time to work together, assign numbers again. Go through this process several times. At the last stage, have all join in a large circle and discuss as a group. This activity provides movement, lots of input, practice, and repetition.

Go through your unit, lesson, or course goals and craft prompts and/or questions and answers accordingly. Use a voice-to-text app to get them on paper. Edit and save for future use/repurposing.

To further reduce the prep and increase student engagement, have them write the questions based on your unit goals. Consider using a format where they can collaborate and can be easily edited (i.e., a Google Doc or large piece of butcher paper). Instruct them that duplicate questions are not allowed.

8

Grammar, Listening, and Writing

In my years of being all about languages, I have truly come to believe that you can never lead with grammar. At the end of the day, we acquire language through comprehensible input (Krashen). With that said, I also believe that having knowledge of how languages work combined with what we acquire equals rapid progress in building real communicative skills.

In line with Krashen's theories, learners tend to move through the same stages with regard to mastery of grammar and structures. It is easy to see this in learners. While we generally teach/introduce simple features (i.e., gender of nouns in specific levels), learners will often still make errors with these at higher proficiency levels. Another example might be working on narrating in the past in a Novice/A-range course—a complex skill not mastered until we enter the Advanced range. It also bears mentioning that the requirements for beginning language teachers tend to be at this same level of skill in some states.

The direct teaching of grammar, listening skills, and writing are some of the more challenging areas of language teaching. In this chapter, we will discuss some effective low-prep activities for bringing grammar to life and some practical ways to make listening and writing less painful.

DOI: 10.4324/9781032622507-13

Lead with Comprehensible Input

Before ever mentioning a rule, demonstrate it in context. Focus on chunks and phrases that will enable them to communicate first before focusing on any rule. Lead with comprehensible input. The perfect time to explain the rule is when learners start to deduce the patterns and ask about the structures.

An example is playing *Guess Who?* with the cheat sheet that has all of the chunks and phrases in context.

To expand, show pictures of people with a short description. Do this a lot before even introducing a rule. Please see this concrete example:

Él es alto.

Deductive Grammar

Practical Ways to Introduce Students to Grammar in Context

1. Essentially, start with any kind of picture. Recognize, listen to the word, and understand.
2. Interact with comprehensible input. Ask lots of questions. Repeat until the students are speaking.
3. Write down the words. Have students match the text to the photo.
4. Take away text. Students write.

Another great way to do this is using the Rassias method. Rassias did these fabulous *micrologues* where essentially you start with a drawing or a photo. The students listen as you talk. Repeat, gesture, emphasize, and make it interactive. Students interact with what you presented, and they produce a product completing the task. Many people now do a version of this called Picture Talk.

Finding a context to provide this input is critical. Your students' presence can provide this naturally. For example, think of a student and describe what they are wearing or some traits they possess. All of the grammar and vocabulary will be in a meaningful context.

Vocabulary is the building blocks of languages. All those words learned can be built up into phrases, sentences, and paragraphs. Clearly, the more words you know, the easier it is to communicate in a new language.

There is this idea that you can learn a lot of words, they start working together, and then we are able to speak a language. This is, on one hand, very much true. On the other hand, it is not true at all. You need to learn words and phrases that are going to stick with you and that are useful. This is difficult when the words you are learning are out of context. The key is *chunking*. This is learning meaningful words and phrases of vocabulary grouped together into chunks.

Consider these words:

- ball
- tomorrow
- I'd
- like
- this

All of these words can be useful. However, memorizing them separately will not be particularly useful. For example, *I'd like*. That is a highly useful phrase. *Tomorrow* is high-frequency and useful. *I'd like this* would be useful. Learning the equivalent of *this ball* in your target language will likely help you learn some grammar rules in context.

156 ◆ Grammar, Listening, and Writing

What's really important is to learn vocabulary that's going to lead you to be able to do something as you learn the new language. Not only does the vocabulary being in context make learning and recall easier, more efficient, and faster, but these chunks serve useful communicative purposes.

Please see these examples of chunking to learn languages:

Rencontres et salutations

Je n'ai pas compris.	I don't understand.
Parlez-vous anglais ?	Do you speak English?
J'ai été heureux de faire votre connaissance.	It was nice to see you.
Comment vous appelez-vous ?	What's your name?
Je m'appelle	My name is........
Comment allez-vous ?	How are you?
Bien.	Good.
Pas trop mal.	So- so.
Vous vous sentez bien?	Are you all right?
D'où venez-vous?	Where are you from?
Enchanté.	It's nice to meet you.
Moi de même.	Likewise.
Où habitez-vous ?	Where do you live ?
J'habite à _____.	I live in_____.

French for Travel and Beginners

| What is your commission rate? | **Quale è la sua commissione?** |

| How much does it cost? | **Quanto costa?** |

| payment | **Pagamento** |

| credit card | **carta di credito** |

| What types of payment do you accept? | **Che tipi di pagamento accetta?** |

| What is the rate? | **Quale è il tasso di interessi?** |

| Is Internet included? | **È incluso Internet?** |

Italian for Travel and Beginners

These chunks serve as great resources to complete tasks. Tasks are, of course, things we do in a language. Gaining competency in tasks to be able to communicate is what we do. Consider curating chunks to share with students to create phrasebooks and dialogues to master specific tasks.

Consider any and every topic you will explore and gamify. Students might do this in pairs, use different colors to match, or connect them with lines. Consider the communicative task you want them to be able to do as you create these. For example, if you want students to be able to talk about their daily routines, write those chunks in context. Students will use the grammar matching activity that you created to complete the task. They can plan to say a set number of things, memorize, and present.

Is it True?

The activity *Is it true?* was presented as a way to introduce vocabulary in the context of students' real lives and interests. Using it to provide input of certain grammatical structures helps make it a reading and speaking activity with grammar in context. For example, if you are teaching a specific verb tense, write sentences using those verbs. See this example in Spanish using preterit verb forms of the verb "ir" (to go).

158 ◆ Grammar, Listening, and Writing

1. Amy fue a la tienda anoche.
2. John no fue a la escuela ayer.
3. Mary fue a casa esta mañana.
4. Ashley y Isabelle fueron a Croacia el año pasado.
5. Jacobo fue al banco el sábado.
6. Todos fueron al estadio el domingo.
7. Julia fue al centro comercial el fin de semana pasado.
8. Jaime fue a la playa hace dos semanas.
9. Lisa fue al restaurante anoche.
10. Emma fue al aeropuerto la semana pasada.
11. Luis fue a la biblioteca anteayer.
12. Rae y Miguel fueron a la iglesia el domingo.
13. Lucas fue a la piscina el sábado.
14. Maisie fue al café el domingo.
15. Megha fue al gimnasio hace una semana.
16. Paola y Scott fueron al teatro el viernes.
17. Cristina no fue al cine anoche.
18. Manuel y Paul no fueron de compras el verano pasado.

Write these based on your students. They first read, respond, and then all review the answers together in this multimodal activity.

Grammar Matching and Mastery Games

Low- and no-prep matching activities can be easily created by writing phrases or sentences on paper in some form. This might be native language/TL phrases and sentences to match on a sheet of paper. These could also be with target language on one side and native on the other. Students match based on your cues, or work in pairs or teams.

#1: Ring a Word/Hear and Circle/Grammar Match

I first learned about this activity from French teacher and author Deborah Blaz as a vocabulary learning activity. I now believe that it is so much more valuable for learning those golden "chunks" that present grammar in context and help people communicate immediately. Consider some of the more difficult structures you work with.

To serve as an example, imagine that you are teaching daily routines. This involves verbs (reflexive in some languages, and often irregular), vocabulary, and transition words. Write these structures in both the target language and native language for students to talk about their own routines. After the matching activity, have them use the TL chunks to report their own routines to you.

160 ◆ Grammar, Listening, and Writing

#2: Verb Charts and Quizzes

Verbs are a major challenge for the learner of some languages. Many speakers give up well before having a sufficient handle to really create with language.

Some dedicated work on verbs and/or structures is necessary. Create charts for notes. Use them as quizzes after working with a verb tense or pattern. I find that it helps with focus, learning patterns early, and using the verbs right away.

Here is an example:

Table 8.1 Verb Chart and Quiz

	je	*tu*	*Il/elle/on*	*vous*	*nous*	*Ils/elles*
parler	parle	parles	parle	parlez	parlons	parlent
adorer	adore	adores	adore	adorez	adorons	adorent
manger	mange	manges	mange	mangez	mangeons	mangent
aimer	aime	aimes	aime	aimez	aimons	aiment
chanter	chante	chantes	chante	chantez	chantons	chantent
travailler	travailler	travailles	travaille	travaillez	travaillons	travaillent
jouer	joue	joues	joue	jouez	jouons	jouent
regarder	regarde	regardes	regarde	regardez	regardons	regardent
rester	reste	restes	reste	restez	restons	restent
donner	donne	donnes	donne	donnez	donnons	donnent

Here are some ways to use verb charts in your classes:

◆ Use as a supplement to the verb activities in your text. Practice makes perfect.
◆ Fill in portions of the chart. Have students complete it in groups using deduction.
◆ Use it as a way to learn patterns. You give them the blank copy. Once they are catching on, they complete it themselves. You check for accuracy, and they have a quiz next class using the same chart. Alternatively, fill in some structures to help them learn the pattern.
◆ Use for communicative activities as a source for questions. Some ideas:
    ◆ Interviews: students use the verbs to create and do Q&A activities.

Grammar, Listening, and Writing ◆ 161

- Hot Seat: put students in groups, and they brainstorm Q&A possibilities for a period of time. They then take turns going into the Hot Seat, asking and answering. Choose one- or two-minute periods. They get a point for each correct Q&A. Students might also write these questions on paper. After editing them, put them in a coffee jar. Students draw questions and chat with the class.
- Use it as a source for verb practice games (board race, write the correct form on white boards, ring the bell if your team knows the conjugation, conjugate before the bubbles run out) or partner Tic-Tac-Toe. Trace and cut out feet on cardstock. Write subjects on the feet. Students walk all over the feet and conjugate the verb you gave them. Try putting the subjects in one wheel and the infinitives in another on a digital spinner, or draw one on the board.

Use the chart as notes, a handout, and/or as the chart to the quiz (see https://reallifelanguage.com/reallifelanguageblog/).

#3: Grammar Auction

This is an engaging, low-prep game.

Start with a set of content and use this game to sneak in some extra study from your text.

Every student draws fake TL bills from a bag, if you have some. Otherwise, assign an amount for all to begin. Decide how much each bid can be, as well as increases in bids.

Write out sentences based on your content set. Some should be correct and some incorrect. If necessary, let them refer to the relevant parts of the text to review the content. This is best done on paper, but text on slides or the board work, too. This activity can be done without writing out the sentences in advance as well. Create as you go.

Students/groups bid on correct sentences. The student/group with the most wins.

This activity works best in groups, but can be individual. There is a lot of talk about what is wrong and how to fix it.

#4: The Error Game

The Error Game is an engaging variation of Grammar Auction. Write down errors from observing and listening to an activity or common errors found at a specific level. These could be from their writing, homework assignments, or speaking. Students have to correct them. You get to do a lot of in-context grammar correction as a game. Incorporate numbers or TL fake money. They get points when they get the correction right or lose for the ones they get wrong.

One important note: students must be comfortable taking risks in your class to play this, which may take some time. Errors need to be treated as essential on the road to fluency.

Table 8.2 Error Game Template

error	correction	points

#5: Dice

This is a fun way to get more verb conjugation practice. Essentially, you take a group of subjects and verbs. Here is a quick visual with some regular and irregular verbs:

Table 8.3 Dice to Practice Verb Conjugations

1 yo	1 hablar
2 tú	2 comer
3 él/ella/Ud.	3 escribir
4 nosotros/nosotras	4 ser
5 vosotros/vosotras	5 ir
6 ellos/ellas/Uds.	6 tener

Have students fill in the verbs in a chart you have made. I haven't listed all of the possible combinations here, but you can if you want.

Table 8.4 Blank Verb Conjugation Chart

1, 2
2, 1
3, 1
4, 4
5, 2
6, 3
2, 2
3, 4
4, 5
2, 6
3, 3

Students would fill in the correct verb forms with any tense you choose.

#6: Battleship-like Q&A

In the classic version of Battleship, students use a chart that visually demonstrates two categories that must be understood when creating with language. For example, gender/number agreement of nouns and adjectives.

164 ◆ Grammar, Listening, and Writing

I learned about this version of Battleship at a conference from Spanish teacher Gretchen Burke, who was kind enough to share an example and explanation of getting students engaging in practice in a specific verb tense.

◆ Step 1: Go over the question and the possible answers from the list. Tell students to secretly choose five activities from the list and copy them on the lines on the bottom left side of the paper. I tell them to cover this area by folding it up so that their partner can't see.
◆ Step 2: Have the students take turns asking the question at the top but with one activity that they would like to guess. Have them mark off on the little lines next to the activity whether the partner answered yes or no. If they answer yes, they are one closer to getting all five and winning. Either way, they need to alternate asking the same question with new activities from the list to find out all five.
◆ Step 3: Once they have found all five activities for each partner (a total of ten), they help each other write sentences in the third person about each other.
◆ Step 4: Repeat steps 1–3 again but with another partner. They will need to write their answers on the bottom right for the second game.

Here is an example of the activity practicing the imperfect tense in Spanish.

1	2	Nombre:_____
		¿Cuando eras niño/niña _____**?**
		Respuestas posibles: **en absoluto** (not at all), **a veces, un montón**
___	___	viajabas en casa rodante
___	___	veías dibujos animados

Grammar, Listening, and Writing ◆ 165

		echabas carreras
___	___	echabas carreras
___	___	jugabas con bloques
___	___	odiabas tomates
___	___	amabas helado de sabor Superman
___	___	merendabas galletas de oreo y leche
___	___	te columpiabas
___	___	jugabas la anda
___	___	te juntabas con la familia los domingos
___	___	hacías travesuras
___	___	jugabas a la casita
___	___	coleccionaba láminas
___	___	remabas en kayak y canoa
___	___	hacías unas escapadas con tus parientes
___	___	jugabas escondite
___	___	saltabas a la cuerda
___	___	trepabas a los árboles

1: Jugué con_____   2: Jugué con _____

Yo_____ a veces/un móntón   Yo _____ a veces/un móntón
Yo_____ a veces/un móntón   Yo_____ a veces/un móntón
Yo_____ a veces/un móntón   Yo_____ a veces/un móntón
Yo_____ a veces/un móntón   Yo_____ a veces/un móntón
Yo_____ a veces/un móntón   Yo_____ a veces/un móntón

Three in a Row

Using a grid, write verbs and subjects. Have students aim to get three in a row.

See example of grid with spaces for prompts and answers.

HEADING

Prompt / Answer	Prompt / Answer	Prompt / Answer	Prompt / Answer
Prompt / Answer	Prompt / Answer	Prompt / Answer	Prompt / Answer
Prompt / Answer	Prompt / Answer	Prompt / Answer	Prompt / Answer
Prompt / Answer	Prompt / Answer	Prompt / Answer	Prompt / Answer

Affirmations

I love seeing so many people embracing positive self-talk and taking steps to help themselves feel their best. Perhaps you have seen people write Post-it notes in places they often see to remind them of their good qualities. While I personally find self-talk most effective when it is done with my own messages, I think it is a clever way to get some input for students that they will see many times. Consider a mirror or other highly visible place to put affirmations in the target language.

Corner Game

Kate Clifton is an MFL teacher, is the author of resources for BBC Bitesize French, and provides professional development for language teachers. She has shared this very active, flexible activity to practice questions and answers, verb conjugations, or vocabulary.

Four students stand in a corner of the room. The teacher asks a question in the target language. The first person to answer moves clockwise to the next corner.

If there is a person there, that person is out and has to sit down. If the corner is empty, the winner moves into the empty corner, but everyone is "safe," and the teacher calls out the next prompt. The winner is the last student in a corner.

The rest of the class should referee who shouted the word out first.

Listening

Listening is one of the most difficult skills in a new language yet so vital for developing language proficiency. As we've discussed throughout the book, much of our natural communication is integrated. For example, one might ask a question (speaking), answer (listening), and take notes (writing). There are numerous skills being used and developed at the same time. Many of the activities in the book are reflective of that, but I want to take a little bit of time just to acknowledge how difficult listening can be without help and share a few strategies to develop listening skills.

From the very beginning of language studies and up through the levels and ranges, comprehensible input is highly important. It just looks different at different levels. If you're teaching a beginning-level class, you may need to use gestures, props, and pictures to create comprehensible input.

With every listening activity, you should, first of all, scaffold. Learners should have a little bit of a background. This is best done with some Q&A and/or visuals.

Next, you want to set the task and explain what they're going to need to do. This is a good time to use that little bit of non-target language that you might have to teach them about the listening strategy.

As an example, for a beginning task, the learner might listen to a short weather report. They might write down any words they understood each time listening to the selection. In the end, they might take the notes that they've written and write a summary.

TL music also makes a great listening activity. Select a song. Google the lyrics that go with that song, and whiteout certain passages. You might select a specific verb tense or specific words. Students fill in the blanks with what they hear.

168 ◆ Grammar, Listening, and Writing

A quick word about listening: we have two ears and one mouth. I try to listen twice as much as I speak. I think this is a great way to acquire language as well as develop empathy.

Listening Labs

Many of us who have experienced traditional language learning have spent time in listening labs. Technology today allows us to access authentic audio as long as we are connected to the internet. Many of the tech tools that we have readily available to us today provide so much help with making input comprehensible. Captions and subtitles are two examples that are readily available. YouTube and Netflix are now language labs. With that said, time dedicated to listening is vital for developing this hard-to-master skill.

Ping-Pong Listening

This is exactly how it sounds. One person says something, then the other one says it back. This can be teacher–class, teacher–student, or student-to-student active listening.

With any of these tasks, you can pair students up and give each other a lot of support in negotiating meaning.

We are so lucky nowadays to have listening labs included with a lot of new foreign language programs. If you don't have it, don't fret. Authentic audio is easily found online.

YouTube Transcripts/Grammar in Context

YouTube videos have transcripts to support language learners. I suggest watching a video, reading the transcript, watching the video again, and then a comprehension exercise. The comprehension exercise can be as simple as circling certain verb tenses or writing three things that happened. This provides deep and rich listening comprehension.

Create simple audio files of daily linguistic tasks. For example, record what you did yesterday, what you'll do later, or where you'll take your vacation (whatever you are working on in class). Play it for students several times. Let them do a traditional dictation, writing down exactly what you said. After a few times, show them the answers. This can be from the transcript generated by your audio.

A variation on this is to bold the chunks you want them to acquire. Extract those parts and provide translations. Have them complete the task, too.

Writing

Writing is the last skill that we develop in a language.

Anyone who has stared at an empty screen or a blank sheet of paper can attest to this. The good news is that our literacy skills are transferable, meaning if we learn them in one language, these same basic skills transfer to our work in other languages.

Some of the very basic work that we did when we were learning how to write was copying, practicing writing sounds that we hear and what the sounds that we hear look like.

The textbook exercises, while often helpful and necessary, are not authentic writing experiences. We could also argue that much of the work that we give in our classes is not authentic because it's not for real communicative purposes. However, these exercises are essential to develop those skills. Not only are they developing writing skills through practice, but they're also building students' language proficiency.

The activities talked about here are not generally interactive. They're not like research projects where some type of input is going to help the students develop some kind of output.

Timed Writing

For beginners, one of my very favorite activities is timed writing. It's quite easy. You give students some support (i.e., a bank of vocabulary words and chunks that they'll need to complete the task). Give them the writing task, a piece of paper, and have them write as much as they can. Tell them not to worry about mistakes. You can always correct those later.

170 ◆ Grammar, Listening, and Writing

Table 8.5 Timed Writing

1. Familia	
2. Nombre	3. Fecha
4. Task: Describe your family. Write as much as you can. Don't worry about mistakes.	
o Familia – Family o Padre – Father o Madre – Mother o Abuelo – Grandfather o Abuela – Grandmother o Bisabuelo – Great-grandfather o Bisabuela – Great-grandmother o Hermano – Brother o Hermana – Sister	o Hijo – Son o Hija – Daughter o Nieto – Grandson o Nieta – Granddaughter o Tío – Uncle o Tía – Aunt o Primo – Cousin o Sobrino – Nephew o Sobrina – Niece

Once students have had some experience with doing this, you can practice the same skill with fluency writing. Set a timer for seven or eight minutes (not too long, not too short), and they write about the topic. They don't get any help. You help them build their skills by filling in gaps later.

Here are some examples of exit tickets and short writing assignments to practice the skill that you practiced in class:

◆ Write a short dialogue with two people meeting and greeting.
◆ List all foods that you remember from today's lesson.
◆ Write a short note in Spanish telling me about yourself.

Students can also do these in a journal. It serves as a great document on progress.

Grammar, Listening, and Writing ◆ 171

Poems

Poems serve as a light activity to practice structures and can even be done by beginners with a framework and access to the vocabulary and grammar they might need.

Here are several poem structures for beginning classes:

#1: Biopoem
Line 1: Your chosen person's name/you
Line 2: Three adjectives that describe the person/you
Line 3: Important relationship or role of the person/you
Line 4: Four things the person loves/things you love
Line 5: Three feelings the person experiences/things you feel
Line 6: Three fears the person has/your fears
Line 7: Accomplishments or achievements of the person/yours
Line 8: Two things the person wants to see happen or become/your future
Line 9: A brief message to the reader about the person/you

#2: Haiku
Line 1: five syllables
Line 2: seven syllables
Line 3: five syllables

#3: Cinquain
Line 1: One single word (the title)
Line 2: Two descriptive words (adjectives) about the title
Line 3: Three words about an action related to the title
Line 4: Four words expressing a feeling or observation about the title
Line 5: One word that refers back to the title

Consider the linguistic task you want learners to be able to do and infuse that into the poem. Starting with similar products from the TL culture is a great way to provide input and examples before students write.

Emails and Letters

Emails and letters are irreplaceable for building skills and practice for real-world communication. Many schools have quite a few rules regarding use of email, with good reason. Students practice *their* language, using digital tools available in email to fill in the gaps. Doing old-fashioned letters helps foster this and practice those same skills.

Have students write their names on slips of paper and put them in a bag. Everyone draws a name and writes a letter.

Ranking Activities

Ranking activities are powerful because they require a lot of thought. Used with reading or listening, they can aid with comprehension and provide opportunities to review vocabulary.

#1: List 15 items in a category

For example, 15 school subjects, 15 foods, 15 places. Students need to select their top three from the list and explain why they are their favorites. They also need to select the last three and explain why they dislike those things.

#2: Predictions

This is a fun one. Students can write predictions about anything of interest. It might be their life, the life of several of their classmates, or future outcomes of any kind. This could be sports, world trends, or summertime, students select whatever theme and write down their predictions.

Graphic Organizers

Graphic organizers can turn a blank page into an interactive rich activity where students practice the vocabulary and grammar that they're learning in an interesting context. Examples are provided in the book that can be adapted to your needs. They develop listening, reading, speaking, writing, and cultural competence.

There are several in the online Appendices section.

Comics

Make comic strips for some engaging learning in class. Try an online generator. Check out <u>www.makebeliefscomix.com/ Comix</u> to get started.

Tech not available to you? Consider drawing a simple strip (or use the Storyboard template included).

100-Word Writing Prompts

As students are building into and through the Intermediate/B level, they need richer prompts than what works for beginners. Find three sets of examples of prompts for a 100-word writing assignment for French, German, and Spanish.

These prompts were generated using artificial intelligence (ChatGPT) and edited. Try these, or generate your own set of high-interest writing prompts for students of all levels.

French:

- ◆ Write an article about your favorite city in the francophone.
- ◆ Write a letter to a French-speaking pen pal discussing your interest in their culture.
- ◆ Describe your dream vacation to a country in the francophone.
- ◆ Write a recipe for a classic French dish.
- ◆ Write a review of a French-language film or book you've recently read/watched.
- ◆ Write a story about a day in the life of a French-speaking student.
- ◆ Discuss the importance of learning a second language in today's society.

174 ◆ Grammar, Listening, and Writing

- ◆ Write a postcard to a friend back home describing your adventures in a French-speaking country.
- ◆ Discuss your opinion about the education system in a French-speaking country.
- ◆ Describe a festival or celebration in the francophone you would like to attend.
- ◆ Discuss the benefits of living in a bilingual society.
- ◆ Write an opinion piece about the effects of globalization on the French identity.
- ◆ Describe a typical breakfast, lunch, or dinner in a French-speaking country.
- ◆ Write an essay about the importance of preserving French heritage and traditions.
- ◆ Discuss the role of technology in the French-language classroom.
- ◆ Write a letter to the French government discussing ways to improve the tourism industry.
- ◆ Write a diary entry about your experience of learning French.
- ◆ Explore the relationship between France and its former colonies.
- ◆ Discuss the impact of the internet on the French language and culture.

German:

- ◆ Write a letter to a friend describing your recent vacation in Germany.
- ◆ Create a brochure promoting a particular city or region in Germany.
- ◆ Write a blog post discussing your favorite German musician/band and their impact on the music industry.
- ◆ Describe your typical day in Germany, from waking up to going to bed.
- ◆ Write about your dream job in Germany and why you hope to pursue that career path.
- ◆ Create an advertisement for a new German product or service.

Grammar, Listening, and Writing ◆ 175

- Write a short story set in a German town or city.
- Describe the German school system and how it differs from your own country's school system.
- Write about traditional German holidays and celebrations.
- Discuss the role and influence of the German film industry on the world stage.
- Write a review of a German book or movie you recently read or watched.
- Describe your experience learning German and some of the challenges you faced.
- Write an essay about the history of Berlin and its significance in world events.
- Explain the importance of recycling and environmentalism in Germany.
- Write about the music festivals and concerts that are popular in Germany.
- Discuss the unique flavors of German cuisine and your favorite German foods.
- Create an itinerary for a week-long backpacking trip through Germany.
- Write about German fashion trends and styles.
- Discuss the impact of German industry and technology on modern society.
- Write a persuasive essay on why more people should learn German as a second language.

Spanish:

- Describe your dream vacation in a Spanish-speaking country.
- Write a story about a day trip to a local town in a Spanish-speaking country.
- Write a letter to a Spanish-speaking pen pal introducing yourself and your interests.
- Describe your daily routine in Spanish.
- Talk about your favorite Spanish holiday and the traditions surrounding it.

176 ◆ Grammar, Listening, and Writing

- ◆ Write a review of a Spanish-language movie or book you recently enjoyed.
- ◆ Write a persuasive essay about why learning Spanish is important.
- ◆ Describe a traditional meal in a Spanish-speaking country and its ingredients.
- ◆ Write a postcard to a friend recounting your experiences on an excursion in Spanish.
- ◆ Write a report on a famous landmark in a Spanish-speaking country.
- ◆ Write a short story in Spanish about your favorite childhood memory.
- ◆ Talk about your favorite Spanish-speaking musician or band and their impact on Spanish culture.
- ◆ Write a comparison of a grammar rule in Spanish and English.
- ◆ Write a poem in Spanish about love or friendship.
- ◆ Write a speech in Spanish describing your hometown and its attractions.
- ◆ Write a dialogue in Spanish between two friends discussing weekend plans.
- ◆ Imagine you are a teacher and write a lesson plan for teaching Spanish basics.
- ◆ Write a news article in Spanish about a current event.
- ◆ Write a review of a restaurant you recently visited.
- ◆ Write a letter to a Spanish-speaking celebrity explaining why they inspire you.

Reference

Blaz, Deborah. *Foreign Language Teacher's Guide to Active Learning*. United States, Eye on Education, 1999.

9

Culture

Culture and language are inextricably intertwined. We want students to develop interculturality. We must expose students to the products, practices, and perspectives of the cultures of our target language. What do they make? What do they do? How do they see the world?

It takes thousands of hours of interacting with the target language and culture to hit the Superior range (ACTFL) in languages that are easiest for speakers of English. As learners work toward that range, they are building their intercultural skills—a vital component of learning to communicate with speakers of other languages.

In this chapter, we will explore activities that can be adapted to any language and level of proficiency that teach language and culture in tandem. A few examples:

Table 9.1 ACTFL's Products, Practices, and Perspectives

Products	Practices	Perspectives
Blogs	Holidays	Religion
Literature	Meal Times	Politics
Food	Dress	History
Music	Ceremonies	Geography
Art	Dance	Gender Perspective
Films	Social Customs	Linguistic Perspective
		Economic Perspective

DOI: 10.4324/9781032622507-14

Big C and Little c

It is also important to acknowledge Big C, little c, and how they work together to build skills to communicate effectively in other languages.

Big C (art, architecture, history, etc.) is high-interest and important. Small c (daily life, such as transport, ordering meals, and greeting) should guide your choices. These are some of the most time-consuming yet rewarding jobs we have as language teachers. Creating experiences and curating materials to provide as input is not always easy. In order for language experiences to be effective, finding the intersection of proficiency level, target language, interest, task, and theme will be unique to groups and individuals.

Table 9.2 Examples of Big C and Little c

Examples of Big C	Examples of little c
Art	Realia
Dance	Shopping
Architecture	Transportation
Holidays	Ordering in a restaurant
Museums	Current popular music
History	Getting around
Literature	Interacting with members of the TL
Poetry	culture
Film	Commercials
Theater	

The two C's work beautifully together. Big C can easily develop those everyday little c skills. One might have students research different works of art and share descriptions of their piece. A student might read a poem in the target language and then write one of their own. Learners might research a holiday in the TL country and compare it to their own. It is easy to see how to create experiences for students that expose them to culture while involving all three modes of communication.

When creating high-quality experiences for students, the right tasks must be designed and created with the right input. This often involves searching for authentic materials and making them immersive and engaging. This might mean finding a great high-interest article as input for argumentative work or finding a guest speaker with expertise on a particular region or subject. These also need to have that sweet spot: the intersection of communicative tasks, proficiency level, and cultural objectives. Since that varies among language and level, it is only realistic to build up your repertoire over time. Some favorites that can be adapted to different languages and levels.

- ◆ TL magazine websites. Students select one article that interests them. They read it and summarize it for the class. This might be horoscopes, recipes, celebrity news, or sports.
- ◆ For a beginning class, their task might be to find promotional materials and extract a few details. A more advanced task would be to find two articles and synthesize the information. They might also find an article on a controversial subject (we give them the keywords) and they argue for or against the position.
- ◆ As of this writing, transcripts often come with videos on YouTube. Students can find specific structures, demonstrate their comprehension, and also complete a task.

More Practical Ways to Infuse Culture in Your Class

Music

As much as I love music and consider it important, I don't believe that it's always the best way to learn spoken everyday language. However, it's a great way to learn about culture and vocabulary. Authentic materials are made by native speakers for native speakers, so music is a powerful tool for infusing authentic materials into your curriculum.

180 ◆ Culture

Music can also be quite effective in making connections. It makes words and phrases melodic to aid in remembering them. Some practical ways to use music in your class:

- ◆ **Sounds and structures.** Songs are essentially poems, and they don't always make a lot of sense at first. With that said, there are lots of sounds, structures, vocabulary, and culture that can be taught and practiced through songs.
- ◆ **Total physical response and immersion.** Some ways to use songs are through dance tutorials. They are immersive ways to learn languages. Students can learn merengue, salsa, sevillanas, and flamenco through immersion.
- ◆ **Interact with TL culture with playlists.** Playlists of useful videos from YouTube for tutorials and songs makes finding them easy. Play them in the background. There's an abundance of ready-made playlists on Spotify and YouTube for learners of many languages. Students can make their own playlists, too. Keep the criteria simple. For example:
  - Create a slide.
  - Find five songs that are school appropriate.
  - Link them to the slide.
  - Include the title, the artist, the genre, and what you like about in the target language.

- ◆ **Grammar and vocabulary.** A very old-school activity is a cloze activity. Take the lyrics to a song and find a structure that you want to teach. For example, Shakira sings *Antología*. It has a lot of preterite, a real struggle for students of Spanish to master. Go through and white out every time there is a preterite verb. The students have to fill in the blanks. Listen a few times. It's a great way to learn that verb tense.
- ◆ **Communicative tasks.** While not authentic, there are some rich, fun, and engaging songs specifically for learners of languages. The songs are catchy and written to aid the acquisition of language. Spanish teachers will know

Sr. Wooley and the *Sing, Laugh, Dance* series in Spanish and French.

In an early stage of this project, I was challenged to find more ways that teachers effectively use music that I hadn't considered. Some further ideas:

◆ Write thoughts and feelings that the song evokes in the target language.
◆ All students write words they hear. Use this to build comprehension as described in the section on listening.
◆ Cut up the lyrics and have students put them in order.
◆ Use music to activate a theme, infusing culture.
◆ Use music as a topic for research. They might write a short report on an artist they like and share it with the class.

Blogs and Realia

Consider how American culture can appear abroad. One such example of American culture abroad is McDonald's menus. What is most interesting is that the photos and pictures make it easy for students to read in the target language. They get an idea about currency and, most importantly, they get great insight into culture at the same time. For example, in Korea it's often the case that the same types of foods tend to be eaten at all meals instead of something different for breakfast as we see in many Western countries. That's reflected in the menu in McDonald's. There are also a lot of specialty items. Students also get great insight into culture by seeing things like Halal chicken Big Macs if you're studying French because of the large Muslim community in France. A simple Google search will bring these items up. Use them as input for chat and a quick compare and contrast for your class.

Blog posts provide insight into the TL culture. If these are not readily available to you, I suggest finding four or five TL magazine websites. Many publish articles regularly for either content marketing purposes or traffic. While it may initially take time to curate articles that are high-interest and appropriate, it is well worth the effort. For novice/A-range learners, you may be simply sharing an advertisement or television schedule which can serve as a source for a short class chat.

Literature, Film, and Art

These activities have existed in language classrooms for as long as I am aware and with good reason. Secondary classes might not have the time to complete a novel like *Don Quijote* or *Lazarillo de Tormes*, and many may not have the language proficiency level, but some exposure to the masterpieces is important in building intercultural skills. Poems can serve this purpose well. Much work is in the public domain and readily available for free.

Film is important but is not low prep when you consider the need to vet. People are constantly curating and updating lists of school-appropriate movies.

Art provides opportunities for all levels of languages. Some examples:

- ◆ Novice learners can do short presentations of a work of art using and recycling basic communicative vocabulary.
- ◆ Portraits: Novice/A-range learners can listen to you describe a portrait and draw it or recreate it as a TPR activity.
- ◆ Intermediate learners can find a work and write a biography of the artist.
- ◆ Upper-intermediate and Advanced learners can research several works from an artist and report on the historical context.

Exercise

Movement is so important. Teaching foreign language gives us lots of opportunities to get exercise and language teaching into the same activity. Exercise videos are available in many target languages. They provide insight into authentic culture. Students find content such as this entertaining as well.

One of my discoveries during the pandemic is world walks. After my trip to Buenos Aires scheduled for April 2020 was canceled, a quick YouTube search showed me some walking videos of the city. There are videos showing streets and neighborhoods of our TL countries. Learners can walk in place to the video for actual exercise, or play it for a few minutes in the background.

Community Service

One of the most unexpected and rewarding things that I've gotten out of being able to speak languages is being able to help people when I didn't expect to be needed. This has gone to helping people who were lost, helping translate, and helping people in an emergency. Finding a way to incorporate this community service is a way to get people speaking the target language outside of class. This might be in the form of students teaching lower levels or offering translation help or language exchange. The experience will provide great insight into the TL culture and perspective.

Travel Abroad

Travel opens the mind and expands the brain. Going abroad can be a lot, but it's certainly worthwhile. I do realize that this is difficult to do in many circumstances due to money and/or family commitments; however, travel is a great theme and context to build language skills at any level, as well as cultural awareness.

This topic is one of my biggest joys *and* biggest source of frustration and investment of time. In an ideal world, input would be authentic, comprehensible, and readily available for teachers to integrate into their classes. Since the goal is to curate materials for optimal language experiences, the teacher knows what the students need and will find engaging. My language experiences that I can share with others gives me the perfect excuse for this.

Don't Reinvent the Wheel

Collaborate with others and be realistic about the time available to invest in finding these materials. The internet makes this all so much easier. Students research projects, foods, travel, YouTube, online articles, blogs, and guest speakers, and add music in the background to provide authentic cultural input that can be made comprehensible for students.

Putting it All Together

A few important things to consider when planning your activities:

CULTURE AND LANGUAGE

LANGUAGE AND CULTURE ARE LINKED	INVEST TIME IN INPUT THAT TEACHES CULTURE
SEEK TO UNDERSTAND	UNDERSTAND THE CULTURE TO TALK WITH ITS PEOPLE
LEARN WHAT PEOPLE MAKE, DO AND HOW THEY SEE THE WORLD	FIND SIMILARITIES AND DIFFERENCES

Reference

BBC Learning English. *The teachers' room: Using songs*, 25 May 2017. YouTube. www.youtube.com/watch?v=iWBofOMDOHQ. Accessed 12 December 2023.

10

Centers, Stations, and Choices

Centers and Stations

Centers are commonplace in elementary school classrooms. They provide opportunities that are student-centered, foster lots of engagement, and can be used to learn anything. Learners focus on a specific skill in a learning center. Centers are great for review and refinement.

Stations are places where learners work on tasks simultaneously. There are differences between the two concepts. For our purposes, we'll consider how to use centers and stations—essentially, places for students to engage in language work with a small group of people—to help students develop skills, proficiency, and stay engaged.

From my experience with younger students, centers were one of my favorite things to bring back to secondary language teaching. Centers and stations provide lots of opportunities to master vocabulary and grammar. With a bit of initial prep, they can provide great opportunities for students to develop skills. You're available to answer questions, problem-solve, and facilitate the activities.

The variety of activities and the time spent engaged in language experiences and tasks helps build that proficiency level. More time engaged = more language. More language = higher proficiency levels.

Organize your centers/stations based on how much time students have available to spend in each center and how many

DOI: 10.4324/9781032622507-15

different activities you want them to do. For a class of 90 minutes, you might have four or five different centers for students to rotate through. These can also be offered as choices when another task is complete.

A few ideas that work with any set of grammar or vocabulary that you're doing:

◆ Pictionary: Use your chapter vocabulary or a relevant list/resource.
◆ Charades: Use your chapter vocabulary or a relevant list/resource.
◆ Hangman: Use your chapter vocabulary or a relevant list/resource.
◆ Reverse Pictionary: Students can also play in small groups with whiteboards or recycling paper.
◆ Grammar Matching Activities: Consider Ring a Word. Choose according to your communicative targets. Students can work in groups, matching TL and native language sentences.
◆ Crosswords: Good for engaging, quiet practice.
◆ True or False: Fun, CI reading. Fill in with your students' names, read and discuss.
◆ Find Someone Who…: Fun communicative activity to find people who have done specific things.

I have heard of teachers breaking this down even further with one skill or one short set of words. One station might be to spell the words. Another might be quizzing each other on flash cards. Another might be using the words in sentences. The last might be translations.

Centers and stations are extremely effective for teaching more difficult concepts. This definitely requires a bit of planning the first time, but the ease and effectiveness of the lessons that you can use year after year is well worth the effort.

For example, consider daily routines. At one center, the students listen to a recording you made (or found on YouTube) about daily routines. Generate a transcript. Learners find specific language from the transcript to talk about daily routines and use it to write their own.

At another center, they could be doing a verb matching activity. They could also be playing Quizlet to practice the verbs relevant to the task.

At another center/station, students are watching tutorials on reflexive and present tense verbs and taking notes.

Students spend about 20 minutes at each center/station. Provide them with a crossword puzzle for further practice and/or for early finishers.

Students are active and learning, and you are moving around the room as a facilitator, helping problem-solve and answering questions as needed.

¿Tomas...?

1. Ask your classmates what classes they are taking (¿Tomas…?).
2. Write the name of someone who takes each class in each box.

Table 10.1 Find Someone Who…

Química	Cálculo	Arte
Música	Biología	Álgebra
Geometría	Inglés	Música

Choices

Essentially, use any other activity that has students getting input in your target language that you have created.

If you want to have some things for those who finish early, consider creating a choice board listing these activities. Create a simple slide with a box for each choice. I suggest copying and pasting from your fast, no-/low-prep repertoire of activities you have ready to do with no notice. Fill in with the choices and change as needed.

Sometimes teachers like to provide more structure in choices. They might create categories and allow students to choose a certain number of each.

There are examples of both kinds described in the Appendices.

Choices can also be allowed for any type of output product. Some may want to showcase their drawing skills. Others may enjoy writing, while others have graphic design skills. Brainstorming possible end products will help students demonstrate their knowledge with a product they enjoy creating.

Game Night (or Day)

Remember those activities we talked about to create centers and instant games? Rename it Game Night (or Day). Fun, engaging language learning and review will continue in the context of your special event. Game Night (or Day) is a sneaky way to get review, engaged study, collaboration, and social interaction into what looks like fun and games.

The concept is, of course, simple. A group of people gather and play games. It may be cards, a board game, or a strategy game. For the language teacher's purposes, these games would be strategically chosen for your learning objectives. For example, you might be reviewing before a test after students have worked on talking about clothing and fashion. Curate your games, such as Bingo and Pictionary to review clothing, and a board game to review numbers. Students might be able to select the games they play or cycle through them all.

In the UK, pub quizzes are quite popular. Have students help prepare questions about the material being studied. The teacher can serve as editor and MC.

Game Night (or Day) might look like fluff on the surface, but with planning, students are being provided TL input and communicative experiences, and enjoying themselves while acquiring the target language.

11

Video and Drama Activities

As I've shared, one of my degrees is in theater arts. As an undergraduate, I double-majored in theater arts and in foreign languages. There are so many parallels between these disciplines.

When a learner has enough words and phrases memorized, they move from the Novice/A-range to the Intermediate/B-range. Many of the resources we use regularly in language classes can be transformed into engaging language experiences using drama.

There are some fun ways to do this in your class. Obviously, you're not going to write or produce a full-length feature. Who would have time for that? But there are some mini takeaways to do that are communicative, effective, and fun, and bring a bit of Hollywood to your class.

Drama

Get the Part

One of the things I think is most valuable about scripts (in our case, that's often going to be dialogues) is that actors have to learn a script. As we know, we hit the Intermediate/B-range when we can create with language. Learning those "scripts" can help accelerate progress.

DOI: 10.4324/9781032622507-16

#1: As a beginner in a new language, you need to acquire words and phrases. To move out of this range and toward fluency, you need to have enough words and phrases to begin to make your own sentences and express your own thoughts.

Actors know how important memorization is to get a chance to work. The monologue is the perfect place to start. I would advise a drama student preparing a monologue from Shakespeare to watch several on YouTube so that they can hear the intonation and pronunciation and replay it enough times to accurately mimic it themselves, then Google the text to memorize their own delivery. I would advise the same to anyone serious about learning a language quickly. You can find your TL word for *monologue*, search YouTube for videos from native speakers delivering monologues, and get started on your own.

#2: The same holds true for poems. Google, watch, memorize, and learn. You will find that the words really stick. This is such a great way to infuse culture and build communicative skills.

Rehearsing for a Role

In a play, an actor must know their lines so well that they are able to ad lib when something doesn't go right. And for language classes, I think of the scripts as being our dialogues in the books or the tasks we are working to master. Students can take those and make a radio play, expand on it, and make a situational dialogue or perform the dialogue in front of the class. All that memorization is going to build into fluency.

Reader's Theater

For Intermediate students, if you've got something longer, like a story, make it into a reader's theater. These are great because you don't have the pressure of memorization, but you do have to delve deeply into what's happening in the story. The students get lots of input and practice with pronunciation. It's a really fun activity. You can add some sound effects, too (https://app. soundstripe.com/sound-effects).

Complaints

In life, we sometimes need to complain in order to right a wrong. These types of contexts make for perfect opportunities to develop fluency, accuracy, and experience in these often-complicated situations (linguistically and socially) that require the ability to be descriptive, persuasive, and firm as well as polite and tactful at the same time. On top of all of these wonderful things, they can also be thoroughly enjoyable.

These types of activities are generally only appropriate for Intermediate/B-range students, as they need to create with language. At this level, students need exposure and practice with advanced structures in order to eventually develop skills in that proficiency range.

Provide students with the context as well as the language chunks, phrases, and structures that they'll need to fulfill the task. In Spanish, this might be using command forms and the phrases with the subjunctive accurately.

One example of what this looks like in practice is during a meal at a restaurant. Learners practice the words and phrases that they would need to persuade the manager to rectify different problems a guest might encounter.

Students take turns playing people who work at the restaurant and diners. Some props to bring the scenario to life: a plastic mouse or spider, a plastic rat, and some sound effects. After practicing what they would say to resolve each situation, put the props in a bag. The "diner" selects a prop and asks to get resolution to their "problem."

Consider making the activities below speaking and listening only. Some added benefits to doing it this way is that learners build the real-life, much-needed experience of speaking on the telephone in the target language, where one can't rely on gestures, notes, or body language to communicate. Consider using phones or computers with cameras off or placing some kind of divider between speakers.

Additional contexts for complaints:

◆ returning a faulty item at a store (be creative with problems)

Video and Drama Activities ◆ 193

- disputing a charge (make fake bills for students to select from)
- problems at a hotel (use sound effects for noisy guests or crying babies)
- changing travel plans (create reasons for changes for students to draw from)
- persuading a teacher to change a grade (relevant, real-life task)
- explaining how something was broken and making the call to get it repaired.

Subtitles

This is a fun one from acting. It has many variations:

#1: Have students act out a situation from your chapter/unit/task goal. These come from whatever they are learning. This might be ordering at a restaurant, going to the doctor, or meeting someone for the first time.

#2: Have them all prepare a situation. They will act the situations out. They won't use words.

The rest of class writes "subtitles" for the situation.

The situations are acted out again. This time, the students read out the subtitles.

Sound Effects

Other contexts to teach are greetings and taking leave. This doesn't look terribly different from beginners or a review class.

They might need a short lesson at the beginning of the course to do this. We naturally have context to do greetings and take leave when the students enter and leave class every day. Use sound effects to do this. We're so lucky nowadays to live in a time where many of these resources are abundant and easy to find online. For example, get the sound effect files to signify an alarm clock or a rooster crowing. You would say *goodnight*, turn out the lights, and then put on the rooster to signify that everybody wakes up. These fit naturally in a daily routine.

194 ◆ Video and Drama Activities

These also serve as context for reviewing weather and seasons. You can easily find files of different kinds of weather online. For your beginners, you could play a couple of them and say in the target language the weather.

Narration

Narration is one of the most difficult tasks that we learn and teach in foreign languages. It involves so much, such as using a lot of vocabulary, knowing many different ways to express things that have happened in the past, verb tenses and conjugations, and then putting it all together in a cohesive and accurate enough way to convey your intended meaning.

When I first started to learn about language proficiency levels in real-world contexts, I was most surprised that narrating in the past was an Advanced/C-level task, especially considering that these structures are often emphasized in a Novice/A-range course. It usually takes people years to master this, even in languages that are closely related to English. With that said, you need lots of practice to get there, so it is imperative to start early on. Some tasks to build these skills:

◆ Talk about where you went yesterday.
◆ Talk about where you went last weekend.
◆ Talk about where you went last summer.
◆ Talk about what you did this morning.
◆ Talk about what you did last night.
◆ Talk about what you did last week.
◆ Talk about what you did last summer.
◆ Talk about what you ate last night.
◆ Talk about what you ate last week.
◆ Talk about what you ate on your last vacation.
◆ Talk about an exciting vacation you took.
◆ Talk about the best meal you ever had.
◆ Talk about a great holiday meal you have had.
◆ Talk about a great celebration you have experienced.
◆ Talk about a meal you had while camping.

Video and Drama Activities ◆ 195

- ◆ Talk about a meal you had outdoors (i.e., a picnic or a barbecue).
- ◆ Describe an experience in a restaurant.
- ◆ Talk about your life when you were a young child.
- ◆ Talk about the games and activities you used to like as a child.
- ◆ Describe a time you were in an airport.
- ◆ Describe in detail a trip you took. Include the hotel room and the surrounding area.
- ◆ Talk about a time you went to a museum.
- ◆ Describe a time you went to a concert. Give as much detail as possible.
- ◆ Talk about a time you went shopping. Provide as many details as possible about the day. Include what you were wearing, where you went, what you bought, and how you felt.
- ◆ Talk about a movie you have seen.
- ◆ Talk about something you heard on the news recently.

Word Story

#1: Take a bunch of words and phrases from whatever communicative task/chapter/unit that you're doing. For example, language for talking about things that have happened in the past. Take out the relevant words and phrases. Either have students write them down on index cards, or have them written down already. Hand them out and ask them to use them to build a story. After some practice, they retell the story without the cards.

#2: The Beginning, The Middle, and The End

Give them some phrases and have them build a story. From the beginning (e.g., once upon a time) and the end (and they all lived happily ever after, or equivalent in your target language). I would give them phrases for the beginning of the story, middle of the story, and end, and then add transitions in there. The beginning, the middle, the climax, and the resolution are provided.

Give them some phrases (no more than four or five) and ask them to write their own story, then tell it. You can also combine this with a presentation where one person is actually the narrator and the people in their group act it out. This works

Screenplay

Another low-prep activity that you can do with any content is a screenplay.

I like to share with people that one page equals one minute on the screen. It's a certain kind of format that they use. It's simple—Courier font 12-point. The format and conventions are rigid in the interest of planning accordingly. On Google docs, there's loads of add-ons (https://workspace.google.com/marketplace/app/screenplay_formatter/329481250452).

Do this with those basic communicative tasks. Think about all the different tasks they'll need to do, then they make their own short screenplay on what you are working on in your textbook. Maybe they'll make a two-minute screenplay of going to the airport, for example. This means a short, focused piece of only two pages or so.

Consider common themes and tasks, such as going to the train station, going to a restaurant, or meeting and greeting, as the content of their film. They have their script edited by you.

They can read it out as a reader's theater when it is done. If you are able to share them and actually film them, you have your own film festival.

For Intermediate students, it would really just be the same process but with more freedom, as they can create with language. They adapt short stories for the screen and change something in the setting. Perhaps they take a short story and actually make a screenplay out of it. If they're creative, they can write something on their own. Learners get tons of input by taking the story and making it into a movie.

Set and Costume Design

One of the activities I did in my theater art studies was costume and set design.

When you design, you read the work numerous times. You don't just read it once; you read it several times to understand what's going on. You read it deeply again, and then you read it once more, making notes, until you've really got a vision of what functionally needs to happen. What technology do you need? What are the characters wearing? What has to happen? And then you can get creative after that last run, after you have interacted deeply with the story.

This brings that same idea to learners: digging deep into something and really bringing it to life. Students can describe the costume for the character and the scenes in the target language.

Perform an Extended Play

This can be done with Novice-level students where they all have smaller parts. The repetition required to master a script well enough to perform it for an audience creates the necessity for input and practice and mastery of all of the included structures. As a teacher, you can create multiple casts. To serve as an example, an adapted play (*The Three Little Pigs* in Spanish) is what the students will perform. If each student plays a couple of roles, then the cast becomes interchangeable. You don't have to worry about somebody being absent, the students have gotten lots of input and they've learned different lines.

Fairy Tale Trial

A variation of this that helps take the edge off learning to narrate in the past while working on past tense verbs is Fairy Tale Trial.

Take a fairy tale in your target language. This is most fun when they are familiar. Have groups perform different ones.

After working through comprehension and the structures needed to retell this story (or any) in the past, students get to work on retelling. You might use authentic texts or ones modified for learners of your target language. Consider providing them with slides, costumes, and props.

Use one of the methods to retell the story to the class. They may do a reader's theater, a narrated play, or a dramatization.

On day two, students rewrite the tales they saw the day prior. It might help to have everyone share and chat about the tales.

For example, in Goldilocks, she broke into the home of three bears. In Fairy Tale Trial, the students get really creative and create a scenario around Goldilocks and her breaking into the bears' house, eating their porridge, and sleeping in their beds. She will be on trial for this.

Take some of the students out of the room to play Goldilocks (and her attorneys) and witnesses. The other group plays the jury. The first groups of students have to explain to the jury what happened. You can be the judge.

You can also have students create scenarios within a story. Goldilocks might be a food critic, for example.

Exchange Students

Do various versions of this.

#1: For complete beginners, after they've had a lesson on greetings, use little stickers with students' names on them. They go around the room and introduce themselves to everyone in the class as though they are meeting for the first time (if in reality people are, it's a great ice breaker). It gets some movement into your class as well as creating an atmosphere of community.

#2: When students become more advanced, give them a few questions. Students each adopt a persona from your target language, and they research the answers to questions based on where they're from. For example, they research/create answers about where they live, what time they eat different meals, or what activities they do depending on their culture. They have to memorize the answers to these questions and then come to the party.

For both levels of students, give them some support by putting the questions up on the board in some way. When students are more advanced, give them people to research. This could be authors or people from history. It's much more elaborate, and we encourage costumes. Students do a more extended variation of this and come to the party.

Video and Drama Activities ◆ 199

Hot Seat

Many actors thoroughly research their roles as soon as they get them. The goal is to completely understand the character's history, background, tastes, family, major life events—anything one can imagine—so that the actor can make that person real and three-dimensional. Many questions might be addressing things never apparent in the script, but the actor chooses to use them to flesh out the character and transform black-and-white words on a page to a character so convincing that we can suspend our disbelief and be immersed in a story. Here are some interpretations of this activity in each proficiency range:

#1: Novice

Each student in class selects a famous person from the TL culture. They then answer a series of questions to talk about themselves and memorize all the answers. Next, they sit in the Hot Seat, where the class asks them all about themselves, and they have to answer without notes. This is what actors often do to help them bring a character to life. They add a lot of details to the character's life and background story that might not be in the work itself but helps flesh out a real person who the audience can empathize with. This provides a great context to learn the ACTFL 5 C's through a fun research project for learners.

You can do this project with any theme. Think musicians, artists, people from history. The possibilities are endless. Some example questions to consider, cut, edit, or add to:

- ◆ What's your name?
- ◆ Where are you from?
- ◆ Where do you live?
- ◆ How old are you?
- ◆ When is your birthday?
- ◆ What are you like?
- ◆ What do you like to do?

Learners can be assigned research of famous people from the target culture, periods of history, or even a famous place. The students then must research and be able to answer a set of questions about their person. It is a great opportunity to learn more about the target culture while recycling lots of everyday language. The students can discuss where they are from, their names, the most important thing that happened to them, or what they would like to do in the future. The possibilities are infinite. The audience asks them questions and must take notes in the target language based on their answers.

#2: Intermediate Range

The activity would largely look the same here but would involve more difficult reading and complex questions. For example, an upper-level high school Spanish class might take on the roles of famous people from the history of the Spanish-speaking world. People like Los Reyes Católicos, Marie Antoinette, or other important figures from your TL culture could be researched from a pre-selected group of sites or articles. The responses would require many paragraph-level (or approaching paragraph-level) responses. They also provide many opportunities for students to practice forming hypotheses. For example, students might be required to answer how the world might be different if Columbus had never met Los Reyes Católicos.

#3: Advanced Range

This activity is appropriate for literature classes. The students would select a character from the story read in class (and perhaps the author or genre, country, or any other criteria). They answer a whole series of questions related to biographical information as well as questions about the conflict, genre, historical background, and/or political climate. It lends itself to a deeper understanding of the reading and culture as well as providing opportunities for the students to practice Advanced-level tasks and extended paragraph-level discourse. Intermediate- and Advanced-level students can also compare and contrast throughout. They can also be required to cite their research.

Do writing as an extension. Have students take notes during the presentations and select a couple to write a summary on. This creates a great IPA (Integrated Performance Assessment) out of the project.

You might even consider helping students master grammar with this activity.

Special Event

Plan a special event in which these famous TL culture figures are present. Students select figures from history. Allow them to research their person thoroughly to bring this character to life. Brainstorm the criteria and consider co-creating with students, as well as practicing conversation points for them to prepare before the actual event.

More Dialogues, Skits, Simulations, and Dramatizations

These can (and should, in my opinion) be done at every level, and often. The depth and breadth will vary accordingly. They provide much-needed exposure and practice toward real-life communication. Bring the dialogues in the book to life and/or have learners create their own to fulfill the same tasks. Build simulations to build proficiency and skills for their real-world functions. Allow students to write skits and dramatizations based on communicative tasks.

When students are more advanced (intermediate and beyond), they can create with language.

#1: You can assign out topics of review, and students can create their own dialogues around that. Take a few minutes to brainstorm themes with students. Divide them out, assign topics, and create the dialogues. These not only serve as powerful review activities but are also great icebreakers and ways to build community in your classes.

For Novice-range students, these activities are a fantastic opportunity to practice creating with language and learning/acquiring the words and phrases necessary to hit the Intermediate range.

#2: Taxicab

As a language teacher, much of my inspiration comes from places you'd expect—research, my experiences, and successful polyglots—but I find myself inspired by the less obvious and perhaps mundane aspects of daily life.

202 ◆ Video and Drama Activities

Dialogue OR Dramatization

Title/Topic

- **Person #1**

- **Person #2**

- **Person #1**

- **Person #2**

- **Person #1**

- **Person #2**

Dialogue or Dramatization

In London, the cab drivers are super knowledgeable about the city and can be chatty. In Taxicab, divide your class into teams. Students take turns being drivers and passengers and must speak the target language (they can talk about anything) until they reach their destination. When everyone gets to the destination, debrief about the things said.

#3: Choose your task and what the final simulation should look like. For example, the simulation might be at an airport. Help students with language they'll need for each role. Give them time to practice (lots of learning happens here) and do the simulation. These are even done in defense language programs. It isn't play—it brings the language into their skill set.

A Note for Introverts

If you're not an actor, or you're shy, don't worry. There are roles for everyone in a production. Costume and set designers are essential. Their work requires digging deep into the target language, text, or a play or film and bringing it to life. Using the target language, they have to look closely at the setting of a story and recreate visual aspects. Maybe you want to do a stage adaptation of a piece of literature that you're doing in French, for example, and the students find appropriate examples of the setting to share. They have to do a lot of research and look at a lot of primary sources to complete this. You're getting connections in there, too. Those are a few activities that I did in my days in theater arts. Working deeply with stories as an actor, a director, a writer, and a designer works beautifully for language classes and could easily be adapted to different proficiency levels.

Movie Talk

A popular activity is Movie Talk, where a short clip is selected to produce a lot of language acquisition. Here is a basic set of instructions.

- ◆ Pre-watching:
  - Activate the learners' prior knowledge by asking questions related to the theme. Chat and provide input to help scaffold it for understanding. Think Q&A/pre-teaching vocabulary they will encounter.

- ◆ Watching the clip:
  - Play the movie or video clip.
  - Encourage the learners to actively listen and pay attention to the language used as well as the visual cues and context. Pause often, do more Q&A and input.

- ◆ Post-watching discussion:
  - Share and discuss vocabulary.
  - What was the main message or lesson you took away from the clip?
  - Consider an extension activity, such as writing a summary.

Many teachers are in situations where they are limited in what they can show to students. While there are many valid reasons (students are too young, school norms, time restrictions), Movie Talk is a way to introduce target language films and clips. While it may not be possible to show a film you know would be great cultural immersion for learners, a clip can be a way to immerse students in language and culture and make it comprehensible.

Movie Reviews

#1: Have everyone come prepared to talk about a movie that they liked. This involves lots of past tense. You have to talk about where it took place, what happened, the different characters that were in it, and what they were like.

Everyone sits in a circle and talks for 30 seconds or a minute about their movie. They can give some basic details in a more beginning-level class or lots of details for more advanced classes. The rest of the class takes notes on each movie. After everyone has shared, everyone has to ask one another a certain number of questions about each movie. It's listening, it's speaking, it's communicative, and it's interactive. At the end, people can select a certain number of other movies that they heard about and now want to see, and they can write about that movie.

#2: Students write reviews to share on a classroom wall on programs they are watching in the target language. Co-create a rating system with students.

Movie Night

This can be a real challenge in foreign languages where what's culturally acceptable in those languages is not in the United States. However, with some vetting, it can be done. Bloggers are constantly updating lists of movies appropriate for school and available online.

Video Diaries

Keeping a video diary on a regular basis is an effective way to build skills and document fluency. Record a weekly prompt. Learners respond.

Be realistic with the time investment here. You may only do this a few times the first year you do this. Be okay with that. Consider getting short video prompts from YouTube. These provide learners with input. The technology allows for a lot of much-needed repetition to acquire language.

Use videos with any of the speaking activities outlined earlier. Here are some additional ideas.

Short-Form Videos

There is much to say about TikTok and social media in general. Regardless of your opinions or access to these apps, the short-form style lends itself to engaging review activities. Additionally, Reels, TikTok, and YouTube Shorts all allow for text, helping immensely with comprehension. Students can get input from authentic sources as well as see products from other learners. Perhaps share short videos with students as a warmup or quick tutorial.

Students can create their own videos as well. The strict time limits require being concise and exact. While I am in no way suggesting that students be allowed to roam free online, because it can be dangerous, with close supervision and planning, short-form videos can be a great source of input and output. The reality is that students use these daily. Adapting and keeping them safe is the most realistic way forward.

Video Prompts for Language Learners

Short-form videos are an engaging way to provide students speaking activities as well as serving as formative and summative assessments.

206 ◆ Video and Drama Activities

With the prompts below, you can ideally provide a similar source of input. YouTube has a wide selection. Create your own to serve as an example for years.

#1: A Tour of My Fridge
Give us a tour of your fridge.

#2: My Backpack
Tell us what's in your backpack in your target language.

#3: My Family
Talk about your family.

#4: What Did You Do Last Weekend?
Either provide questions and/or an example of you speaking in your target language about your weekend.

#5: What Did You Do During Your Last Vacation?
Either provide questions and/or an example of you speaking in your target language about your last vacation.

#6: Me
Learners talk about themselves. Assign a specific number of things to say or questions to answer. Consider doing the Review Project as a short-form video.

#7: My Closet
Show us what's in your closet in your target language.

#8: My Neighborhood
Show us around your neighborhood in your target language.

A few years back, I had an opportunity to study with a group of teachers at the Anne Frank House. While there, I learned about a great project they do with schools called the Memory Walk. Essentially, students research the history of their local area and make a video.

#9: When I Was Younger...
Students create a slideshow about their lives when they were younger and narrate it.

#10: News Flash
Provide some input (a news flash or questions) and students give a quick report about it.

More Prompts

Give students a task. Some examples:

- Explain how to go from one point to another in a city using the bus.
- Explain how to go from one point to another in a city using the metro.
- Explain how to go from one point to another using the train.
- Describe things you must do to prepare for a trip.
- Describe things you find in an airport.
- Describe things you find in an airplane.
- Describe what you must do to check in for a flight and get on an airplane.
- Describe a time you were in an airport.
- Describe in detail a trip you took. Include the hotel room and the surrounding area.
- Talk about a city you would like to visit. Research and provide as much detail as possible.
- Talk about a trip you would like to take and why. Talk about what you would like to do on this trip.
- Talk about a time you went to a museum.
- Talk about a painting in detail.
- Talk about different types of art.
- Talk about the types of music you like.

208 ◆ Video and Drama Activities

- ◆ Talk about your favorite song. What is the theme?
- ◆ What is your favorite group? Why? What are they like?
- ◆ Describe a time you went to a concert. Give as much detail as possible.
- ◆ Talk about a movie you have seen.
- ◆ Describe a television show you like.
- ◆ Talk about a time you went shopping. Provide as many details as possible about the day. Include what you were wearing, where you went, what you bought, and how you felt.
- ◆ Describe typical leisure activities on a vacation.
- ◆ Describe typical leisure activities on a weekend.
- ◆ Describe typical leisure activities on a summer day.
- ◆ Describe typical leisure activities on a winter day.
- ◆ Describe different types of television programs.
- ◆ Talk about your favorite actor.
- ◆ Talk about your favorite singer.
- ◆ Talk about your favorite writer.
- ◆ Talk about something you heard on the news recently.
- ◆ Talk about a reality program you have seen.
- ◆ Say ten things you did yesterday.
- ◆ Tell the plot of your favorite book.
- ◆ Tell the plot of your favorite movie.
- ◆ Tell your favorite children's story.
- ◆ Describe an event that happened in your community.
- ◆ Talk about the different people responsible for reporting the news.

Reading Reaction

Consider allowing students to answer questions or respond to reading via video. They might even do a jigsaw activity, with each student/pair/group being responsible for sharing the content of one part of the selection.

Test Review

Short-form videos are a great way to review for a test. Each student is assigned a different topic to provide an expert quick review on. Some ways to do this:

- ◆ Each student provides an expert tip on a specific topic, page, or concept. For example, verb conjugations or words and phrases to complete the communicative task the section is presenting. This might be narrating in the past or talking about a school schedule.
- ◆ Put students in groups. They are then tasked with providing cheat/study sheets of different sections, tasks, or concepts in the section.

Puppet Shows

Puppets are not just for little kids. They are a wonderful tool to get people talking. Consider getting some puppets to perform dialogues and other speaking tasks. Some will find it a great help to overcome shyness. Do as you would for any other dramatization with assigning specific tasks and criteria to bring the black-and-white page to life.

SECTION 6

Students and teachers have awareness of and access to proficiency-oriented assessments and use them regularly.

12

Assessments

We are incredibly lucky as language teachers with regard to assessment. Oftentimes, it's quite simple. Can you say it: yes or no? Do you understand it: yes or no? Can you write it: yes or no? However, we all know the topic is much broader than that, and, fortunately, scales and tools to measure proficiency are becoming more and more readily available with each year.

As simple as assessment can be for languages, I know that many of us have specific requirements in that area. It might be specific category weights (I hate these), specific tests, and/or a prescribed number of grades to take. I have always found it ironic that we are teaching people how to communicate yet are often encouraged to criticize them as they do so. A few tenets:

- ◆ As language teachers, it's important to maximize our time in the target language. Rarely would I suggest giving a large, long test that would take an entire class period for anything below the Intermediate-High range. The assessments should match the language proficiency range. For example, if you're working in the Novice range from absolute beginners up to students starting to come out with their own phrases, your assessments should be short (10–20 minutes long, maximum).

  As they progress to the Intermediate level, they'll be much longer. Think 40–50 minutes to an hour. When

DOI: 10.4324/9781032622507-18

you're preparing for an advanced language level where people are producing paragraphs, your time is going to reflect that. They're going to need a lot of time to read and understand. They're going to need a lot of time to listen to audio sources and video sources and do something with them to start producing paragraph-level discourse. As a rule of thumb, the more they can do, the longer the assessments.

◆ Keep it simple. Give them a task and a thing or two to provide feedback on.

◆ Keep assessments focused on what students can do. Give feedback to help them do what they can't yet do.

◆ Group/in-class work. Group work is critical for language classes. Communicative tasks are the foundation of building these skills.

◆ It's all practice. Practice leads to performance. Performance leads to proficiency. More practice starts the cycle again. This is the key to progress.

◆ Create rubrics with students. Keep them simple and easy to manage for you and the students.

Summative and Proficiency Assessments

We have proficiency targets for ourselves and for our students. In order to meet these targets, formal training in rating language proficiency has been indispensable, as well as experiencing developing skills in other languages.

When I did the journey of purposefully going from Advanced-Low Spanish up to near-native proficiency, it was a long process. I wanted to give up a few times because I thought I didn't understand how I could invest so much time in something and just not succeed. But I finally got there. It was the best learning experience of my life. I was able to adjust my expectations and really understand what it takes to be able to go from the beginning to wherever you want to go.

The ACTFL Inverted Pyramid is one of the most useful tools I have encountered. If you see the pyramid, you'll notice it gets wider and wider. What that means is it takes longer to move through each of those levels. That's an important thing to understand. You can progress quickly through that low Novice range. It's going to take twice as long (even two to three times as long) to progress through each proficiency range.

There are so many tools out there that are readily available to be able to measure fluency. They also help set goals and understand where the goal is in relation to current proficiency. Learning this helps in continuously moving forward without wasting a lot of time.

Quick Check-ins

#1: The Hand
An easy way to do this is to assess with The Hand. This is informal, of course. I like to think of my pinky as words. The next two fingers are phrases and sentences, moving toward Intermediate/B-level. After sentences, we have paragraphs (four fingers). The whole hand represents extended speech.

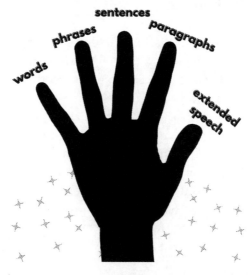

The Fluency Hand

#2: CEFR Can-Do Statements

Another free resource is the CEFR. They have Can-Do Statements that talk about what people can do at different levels of languages. I'm not really sure if they do any formal proficiency testing, but they certainly have a lot of resources. They have it broken down by A, B, and C tasks that will show you what people can do at different levels of languages. It's an extremely useful tool that doesn't cost any money.

Many European countries have their diploma programs to test for evidence of having mastered different levels. They often offer these tests in large cities worldwide via their cultural centers (think Alliance Française).

I highly recommend checking out Language Testing International. If you need an official rating in the U.S., this is the place to go. There is also something called the COPI, where you can get your proficiency tested in several languages.

The ACTFL Can-Do Statements

I think that the Can-Do Statements by ACTFL are a bit more detailed. They also have the Interagency Language Roundtable, which is published by the U.S. Government, and they go much higher than the ACTFL Can-Do Statements. There are also some tests. You can take a telephone interview to measure your language proficiency level and provide an official rating.

While it's a speaking test, it's deceptively difficult. The candidate has a conversation in which the ceiling of ability is assessed.

This section on summative assessments was shared because I think it helps immensely to deeply understand those larger goals. Sitting through at least one formal language proficiency assessment will provide a completely different lens. I do them often in different languages. It helps keep my perspective as a learner fresh.

Some of us will also be required to give summative assessments as well. However, I find formative assessments most relevant and useful since we have time to change course and provide students with feedback.

216 ◆ Assessments

Formative Assessments in Your Classroom

Your assessment should match the proficiency range. In general terms, think of what they *can* do. For Novices, it's words and phrases. Intermediates can create sentences and short paragraphs. Advanced goes from paragraphs to connected paragraphs.

Use the projects and performance tasks throughout the book as they fit into your program. Proficiency- and performance-oriented grading can be a shift. Do what you feel comfortable doing. If doing some traditional assessments mixed with some performance assessments helps you see progress at the same time as keeping the traditional assessments you love, continue to do so.

#1: Exit Tickets

These are short, focused, and can offer a lot of insight into where learners are. An example:

Nombre:

Fecha:

On a small piece of paper, please answer the following questions and hand it in as your exit ticket for today's Spanish lesson on greetings:

1. How do you say "hello" in Spanish?
2. What is the response for "hello" in Spanish?
3. Can you name at least two other ways to greet someone in Spanish?
4. What is the difference between "tú" and "usted" in Spanish?
5. What is one thing you learned or found interesting about Spanish greetings today?

#2: Speaking Tasks

Have them do dialogues, dramatization, improvisation activities, or skits to demonstrate their skills. For Novice students, give them tools to create or specific chunks to learn that help them fulfill a specific task. Intermediates can create with language and can make their own.

#3: Interview

Oral interviews assess where learners have to converse with the instructor or a native speaker. Similar to the formal one shared above, these provide an opportunity to assess learners' ability to use the language and their fluency. I love these because they are easy to prepare, develop real-world skills, and can be built around relevant and high-interest content. Consider the Cháchara Circular or set a specific amount of time in the target language to speak as a class.

#4: Writing

Use fluency writing as an assessment tool. This can be done from fairly early on. Give people a few minutes during which they have to write about a certain topic. Tell them not to worry about anything but try to get their ideas out. Give full credit. For example, "Tell me about your family." They can even list out the people in their family.

A learner who can create sentences might tell you or ask others questions about their family. It doesn't have to be perfect. That same writing activity might look like a strong paragraph a year later. When students are in their third or fourth year and beyond, it's going to look a lot more like an essay.

Give these writing assessments as performance tasks (i.e., homework; write 75 words about yourself, write 50 words about last weekend, write 50 words about your house) and use them as short assessments. For example, "I'm going to give you 9 minutes to tell me everything you can about the future." Be an easy grader. Have certain criteria: no English, only target

218 ◆ Assessments

language. Was it understandable? Make some corrections on it. You can do the same thing with short speaking activities, such as those recorded talks that can also serve as documentation of progress in addition to being effective learning experiences.

Graphic organizers are a great way to organize writing and develop literacy skills. They can also serve as useful formative and summative assessments.

Essay

Topic/Title:

Thesis Statement:

Body Paragraph 1:	Body Paragraph 2:	Body Paragraph 3:

Conclusion:

Name: _____   Date: _____

Essay

Title: _____

- Beginning Details:

- Middle Details:

- Ending Details:

Name: _____ Date: _____

My Story

#6: Tasks

Tasks have been repeated throughout the book for a reason. They are one of the fastest, most useful, and authentic routes to building proficiency in another language.

The American Council for the Teaching of Foreign Languages talks a lot about performance tasks. Essentially, a task is doing something in the target language. It can be as simple as greeting someone or as complicated as giving a speech as the president of that country. Assign tasks; specific, communicative outcomes

220 ◆ Assessments

that you want students to practice and eventually be able to do to build proficiency. For example, use the <u>ACTFL</u> (<u>www. actfl.org/educator-resources/ncssfl-actfl-can-do-statements</u>) and the <u>CEFR Can-Do</u> tasks (www.coe.int/en/web/common-eu ropean-framework-reference-languages/the-cefr-descriptors) as assessments. You might select them or have the students select them. They're great ways to set goals and measure progress.

At every chance possible, authentic tasks and experiences should be used. These can be hard to create in our often artificial setting. Think guest speakers, field trips, community service, and projects. Perhaps the final exam is the class having a conversation for a certain amount of time.

Real-life tasks are one of the most powerful ways to develop skills quickly. However, they don't always fit neatly into our classes.

At Cornell University, their beginning Spanish students engaged in a series of authentic tasks (writing an email to their host family before arriving to study abroad) and pedagogical tasks (tasks meant to practice specific skills). The tasks aligned with their required textbook. This type of assessment aligns real-world communicative objectives and extracts what students are meant to learn to do in the course.

The more tasks a learner can do, the stronger their skills will be in their target language.

#7: Completion

Assign many things for completion in lower-level language classes. If you've asked them to do a certain thing, don't look for perfection. Look for the task to be completed. For example, "Write a paragraph about a time you took a vacation." Mark up the text and make corrections, but don't worry about anything else. If they complete the task, regardless of how well it's done, they'll get credit. They build up enough of that completion and start building the skills and the confidence to do it really well. Essentially, this is pass/fail, and allow them to redo the ones that they failed. Keeping the focus on the feedback to complete the task fosters learning.

If you want to be really specific or particular about certain structures, I recommend pass/fail instead of completion. For example, "Tell me ten things about your daily routine." If a student doesn't do it to your standards, they fail. However, they're welcome to do it over again and as many times as they need. This way, you can ensure that They've learned the structures that you want them to have learned, and they'll do so well. This type of grading might be difficult for students to adjust to at first, but eventually they'll appreciate it because they know that they have the opportunity to revisit anything for which they haven't met the standards.

Do these as oral or written exit tickets, too.

#8: Speaking Work

Assign a lot of speaking work. Keep the work short, specific, correlated to proficiency level, and sweet, without any bells and whistles.

Give students an example of something you want them to talk about. For example, when you're first learning how to talk about the past, "Tell me five things you ate yesterday." That could be a simple oral presentation/speaking assignment.

To give them some help, tell them that they're allowed to have a visual. If it was "What did I eat yesterday?" give them a paper plate that they can draw on and write down the foods that they ate. If it's more sophisticated, such as talking about where a member of their family came from, they can bring in a picture of that person. Allow and encourage them to have visuals to help them speak.

In the lower levels, you'll just have to offer them a lot more support of what that looks like. You don't want them reading off of a slide, but you do want them to have the support that they need.

Graphic organizers are not only a great way to organize what to talk about, but they also serve as great ways to organize research about culture.

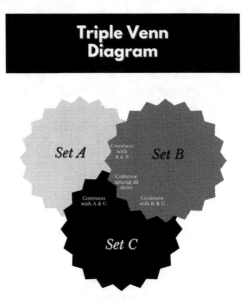

Triple Venn Diagram

#9: Chapter Review

A wise teacher once described traditional chapter tests as nothing more than "tabulations of deficiency." They are bound to make loads of mistakes. I think that they are worth using, but perhaps not how intended.

Sneak in traditional textbook tests and make them opportunities for deep study. This is a good pair or group activity. You can give them the chapter review and tell them they can use any tool they want, except you. There's a lot of community, collaboration, and learning happening. You then give the chapter test in a similar way. This is great when you have more difficult grammatical structures. Again, you're not testing them for mastery; you're sneaking in an opportunity to learn.

#10: Recordings

Consider using any of the recording activities we talked about as assessments. Perhaps they record themselves and provide a short self-assessment. Perhaps they take two recordings and write a reflection on their growth and set a new goal. They can serve as either formative (feedback for further progress) or summative (a final), or a series can serve as evidence of growth over a period of time.

#11: Projects

While many of the projects/activities shared don't fit into the definition of a real problem/project-based activity, I love the idea of these and do know that they can be very valuable. However, they can easily turn into a translated output project without a strong foundation, framework, and structure. They might be better described as immersive activities or mini experiences, as opposed to real projects.

Assign "projects" whenever you can. They can look a lot of different ways. It might be something as simple as creating a menu in the target language or as complicated as working together to research for travel you might be doing. Projects should be relevant, build language proficiency, be enjoyable, and allow students to show and use their passions, interests, and talents.

I am terrible at art. I don't enjoy it, and I don't enjoy drawing (with the exception of doodle journals). However, I believe that a lot of projects should have that as a choice for students who enjoy art, as it is a great way to learn vocabulary. A project might be making a movie, giving a report on the TL country, finding current events in the TL country, learning about the history of the TL country, researching a recipe and making a dish, interviewing a native speaker, or researching a famous work of art or architecture. One of the best things about teaching and learning languages is that the world can be your textbook, especially now with all the resources we have online.

This might not be popular, but I'm going to talk about old-style learning and accuracy. We acquire language. With that

224 ◆ Assessments

said, a fast way to build proficiency in a language is to understand the first of Krashen's Five Hypotheses: language learning/acquisition. Acquisition is what we naturally absorb and acquire, much like we learned our first language. Learning is all the deliberate activities that we do to learn a language. These two together are the perfect marriage.

Give some assessments that call for a great deal of accuracy. Please note that I said *some*, and not a lot. For example, conjugating verbs. This might look like characters, recognizing characters in other languages, or activities that involve reading a script. In these activities, allow students to do them over and over again (on their own time, I suggest) for mastery.

Give them a verb conjugation chart and do some communicative games and activities with it. Their quiz might be to fill in the chart exactly by rote, memorization, pattern, and activity. If they fail, or they want to get a better grade, they are welcome to make it up as many times as they wish. It works, and students master verbs quickly using this.

Modern definitions of project-/problem-based learning can serve as assessments, too. Perhaps a real-life trip to a restaurant, interaction with a native speaker, or other real-world task can demonstrate skill. Consider assigning a set amount of time to speak as a class. Learners do some practice runs to see what they need to master to complete the task.

#12: Games and Play

Don't be ashamed to use a game as an assessment. Early on in my career, I started doing a lot of games because I knew that foreign languages could be challenging for some.

Play games in your class and use them as assessments. For example, Guess Who? (https://powerpointgames.uk/portfolio-items/guess-who). Learners can practice with support, and the assessment is completing the game in the target language without help. Allow them to retake for mastery. This makes it lower risk, allows them to master the task, and keeps the affect low. The quiz can be pass/fail. Don't base it on who wins or loses. They get full credit for completing the task.

Assessments ◆ 225

They are welcome to repeat the task for mastery as many times as they need to do so.

#13: IPA (Integrated Performance Assessment)

ACTFL defines three modes of communication as <u>interpretative, interpersonal, and presentational.</u> Basically, it is understanding (listening and reading), interacting, and one-way presentations (writing and speaking). Much real-world authentic communication fits into these three definitions. As a result, they provide a great framework for building these communicative skills in our classes.

ACTFL, the American Council on the Teaching of Foreign Languages, is a huge proponent of IPAs—Integrated Performance Assessments. These are fantastic opportunities for students to engage in real-life language tasks. IPAs involve using the three modes of communication as defined by ACTFL:

Interpretive: what we understand.
Interpersonal: people are speaking to each other.
Presentational: one-way presentations that are either spoken or written.

IPAs are assessments that involve these three modes.

In real life, this might look like a group of people watching the news, picking up their computer and reading a little bit more about a subject, and then having a discussion about it. It's a natural context. In IPAs, experiences that mimic these are done in a similar context tailored to your students' language level. An IPA you assign might be a topic you want to review or learn for the first time. Students read something, have a conversation about it, and then each present or write a reaction to it.

#13: Portfolios

Portfolios are a collection of learners' work, representing their progress and achievement in different language areas. It can include essays, audio recordings, video presentations, and other learning artifacts. Keep some traditional assessments, too. It is rewarding to see students make progress throughout a course.

Ungrading

Many conversations are happening around grading. Many of us want to focus on the content and learning, not a certain number. Ungrading is a conscious choice to move from number grades and shift the focus back to the learning.

Many argue that grades are also inequitable. These conversations are opportunities for us to focus on creating confident communicators by requiring tasks to be completed to a certain standard with feedback to help get them all there.

References

ACTFL. "Performance Descriptors for Language Learners." American Council on the Teaching of Foreign Languages, www.actfl.org/uploads/files/general/Documents/AppendixN-ACTFLPerformanceDescriptorsLanguageLearners.pdf. Accessed 30 November 2023.

CEFR. "CEFR Descriptors." Common European Framework of Reference for Languages, www.coe.int/en/web/common-european-framework-reference-languages/cefr-descriptors. Accessed 28 July 2023.

ACTFL. "NCSSFL-ACTFL Can-Do Statements." American Council on the Teaching of Foreign Languages, www.actfl.org/educator-resources/ncssfl-actfl-can-do-statements. Accessed 28 July 2023.

Kenyon, Amy. "What Is Ungrading?" Duke Learning Innovation, 22 September 2022, https://learninginnovation.duke.edu/blog/2022/09/what-is-ungrading/#:~:text=Ungrading%20is%20a%20practice%20which, to%20the%20course%20learning%20goals.

ACTFL. "Language Proficiency Testing in 120+ Languages: LTI." LTI, www.languagetesting.com. Accessed 28 July 2023.

Cornell Center for Teaching Innovation. "Task-Based Language Teaching." YouTube, 25 May 2023, www.youtube.com/watch?v=N2yrhgCZa3l&t=26s. Accessed 28 July 2023.

SECTION 7

Members understand that errors are natural on the road to fluency. Accuracy comes later.

13

Professional Development

"Members understand that errors are natural on the road to fluency. Accuracy comes later."

While this statement refers to building language proficiency, it also leads my philosophy toward improving as a teacher. Build a repertoire, leave room for experimentation, and learn from errors as you grow.

Teachers work incredibly hard. Realistically, they have a profound effect on the success of students. Most school districts and organizations require teachers to continue to develop professionally. There are often a required number of credits or hours for us to take. I agree with always growing; however, I do think that the demands can be a lot. Here are some things I have done to keep going over the years.

Professional development can be a loaded topic. There are often so many required activities for teachers to do already. Some courses, required training, and workshops can be greatly beneficial for both teachers and students.

While I can't speak to your specific requirements (i.e., clock hours, credits, etc.), I can share what has been the most valuable for me.

Conferences and Social Media

Language conferences are one of my favorite things to attend to develop professionally. I'm often a speaker at these events. However,

DOI: 10.4324/9781032622507-20

even in putting together a presentation for a group of my peers, I learn a great deal. Then I have the opportunity to see other people's presentations. Check out ACTFL, Language Show, AATSP, AATF, and AATG. Many districts and organizations support attendance.

A word about these conferences: the reality is that as valuable as they are, financial and familial commitments can make attending these difficult. I also believe that as language teachers, the real world is a goldmine of resources. This gets better every day, thanks to the internet.

Get on social media and find a group of teachers. There are so many generous and amazing language teachers who share every day what they're doing. You'll get some great ideas.

Fill Your Cup

I think this one is the most important of all. As teachers, we give. As language teachers, we give, plus we work extremely hard to make difficult content fun and accessible, and ultimately become part of the student's ability to communicate with people from other cultures all over the world.

It's fun, but it's hard work. It's really important to take care of yourself. I work extremely hard to do a good job and get my work done but also do everything I can to not bring home my work regularly. It's important to leave work at a reasonable time and have a life. I'm going to share a few ways to improve your teaching, inspire you, and engage in improving your language skills, if you so choose. You can't give from an empty cup, so it's important for you to fill yours, whatever that looks like.

Not-Do List

I have increasingly become an ardent fan of the not-do list. This often for me starts with a to-do list, where l list all of the things that must be done. Go through and find the things that can be automated. Next, prune. What are things that don't necessarily need to be done? Is my time better spent by hiring somebody to do it for me? Some examples of this might be hiring a cleaner or getting a meal subscription service. You can't do everything. Don't expect yourself to do so. Find ways to find time in your life for you.

Oxygen Mask

After you've done some streamlining in your life, find some concrete ways to make your life easier. These are regular oxygen mask activities. These can be anything that are restorative things to look forward to. It can be as simple as ten minutes of joy in your life every day, but ensure that you schedule it.

Make Your Life Easier Next Year

In Chapter 2 on starting the school year, I discussed routines, procedures, and review. I mentioned author Harry Wong and his emphasis on establishing routines and procedures at the beginning of the school year. Harry Wong, in his presentation, discussed a very effective teacher. He said that this woman spent Friday nights in her classroom, making sure she was prepared for the following week. This allowed her to go home and have a weekend. This really resonated with me, because I see how much work there is for a teacher to do and only 24 hours in the day. The math doesn't always add up. For me, while I did stay late a few Friday nights, what felt a lot more natural to me was spending the beginning of my summer on my Mac and experiencing languages for the remainder. I'm able to feel like I can have a summer and feel uber-prepared through having expanded my repertoire of activities and built my skills.

Engaging in Activities that You Enjoy

Rest, worship, exercise, cooking. What do you enjoy? What restores you? The expectations on us are high, and to be able

Professional Development ◆ 231

to meet them without completely burning out, it's important to keep yourself at the top of that priority list.

Graduate Work

Many of us have specific requirements and will accumulate graduate credits due to them. I value traditional classes and love how flexible online programs provide increasingly effective experiences. With that said, many universities offer summer programs designed specifically for teachers abroad. I did this early in my career and loved every minute of the experience, as well as what it did for my language skills and building my repertoire of experiences for learners.

Language Proficiency

As a native speaker of English, my level of proficiency in Spanish was not always where I wanted it to be. There was a lot of time invested to build a high level of proficiency. While it isn't necessary to teach Novice/A-range learners, it certainly helps. Languages can be cognitively demanding. Add this to teaching, and it can be a tiring day. Investing in building a high proficiency level has made life significantly easier.

Learning other languages has helped me continue to experience languages as a learner. This helps create effective and engaging experiences.

While I love languages, they aren't always easy. It is hard to have the headspace sometimes when you most need it. Finding ways to take care of myself so I can do for others and fit languages into my routines drives the professional development activities that I choose.

#1: Reading

Reading is probably one of the best ways to improve your language proficiency skills. Dr. Stephen Krashen did a study of two hyperpolyglots, one of whom never lived outside of his native Hungary. He spoke numerous languages and did so by doing all of his pleasure reading in a foreign language. Doing this regularly can help you build up to near-native proficiency as well as find great activities for students in reading in your target language.

#2: Audiobooks

We talked about audiobooks in Chapter 6. I am mentioning them again because they are such a valuable resource for building language skills. Audiobooks have been a way for me to read when I can't "read." Teachers are busy people. Eyes get tired from teaching, grading, and reading emails all day. Audiobooks are a way to continue to consume content and books for pleasure, personal development, self-improvement, inspiration, and building language skills.

#3: Walking

I love the endorphins that you get from the gym or a great hot yoga workout; however, walking is probably the most sustainable exercise around.

As teachers, we walk around our classroom, but we also spend a lot of our planning time sedentary. Walking regularly is a great way to get in some movement and reduce stress. I love to combine this with my audiobooks. One summer, when I was on the cusp of hitting my near-native language proficiency in Spanish, I walked every day, twice a day, listening to audiobooks in Spanish, really focusing on deep understanding. I lost weight, reduced my stress, and hit my goals. Audiobooks are available in all levels of many languages.

#4: Develop Language Proficiency Through Binge-Watching

Another way to develop professionally in terms of improving your language proficiency (if you are looking to do that, as well as finding activities for your students) is to binge-watch. I am astounded at what's available online now. We can watch entire series in our target language. The technology provides great support, such as subtitles and closed captioning. Get on YouTube and start searching for content that you would enjoy. Think reality shows, telenovelas, documentaries, series, and drama. Check out Yabla—specifically designed for language learners with games, captions, and a patented player. Netflix has content from all over the world, too.

#5: Learn Something You're Curious About

My best language learning activities have become my most effective experiences as a learner of both languages and new things in general. Learning things that are seemingly unrelated to languages can really help you develop professionally. For example, learning how to make a simple video or make an MP3 file can then be something that's easily incorporated into your lessons and serve as a useful tool to help students make projects and document their progress. This rolls over into pleasurable activities. A few examples: learning how to publish, graphic design, photography, cooking, an exercise routine, painting, or playing the guitar. While these should be kept for yourself and your own personal development, they can help make you more capable of delivering more dynamic lessons, as well as incorporating things you and students enjoy into your lessons. More engagement = more learning.

#6: Guest Speakers/Individual Lessons

We talked about guest speakers, where you can find native speakers for student projects. If you do this, you know it is a great way to connect with speakers of the language that you are learning.

One of my favorite activities for improving my skills to teach languages is to continue to study languages. I get my best, most effective, and most engaging activities from these independent studies.

234 ◆ Professional Development

This particular resource is an absolute gem. Italki allows you to connect with native speakers all over the world for individual language lessons. It differs from language exchange in that the lesson is completely focused on your learning.

Italki has teachers from all over the world, as well as something they call *community tutors.* Essentially, these people don't have any teaching qualifications but can offer conversation practice. I see this as a tool to practice communicating (we can study grammar on our own), so their credentials to teach languages is not terribly important to me personally.

Being able to speak with native speakers from anywhere is great professional development. Imagine being able to improve your skills and confidence without needing to travel.

We learn languages by understanding and build our skills through practice. Communicating in the target language provides the perfect opportunity to get the input we need to understand and build vocabulary and learn grammar in context. Speaking with native speakers also offers the opportunity to practice and continually test yourself, leading you to fill in the gaps of any language you don't know. These skilled native speakers are used to working with learners, so they know how to provide comprehensible input to learners and are the perfect supplement in your classroom to teach languages.

I couldn't travel in 2020. Instead, I supercharged my Italian with italki. Not ideal, but it is a serious option to build skills from anywhere.

Here is a list of my questions for beginners:

- ◆ What's your name?
- ◆ Where do you live?
- ◆ Where are you from?
- ◆ When is your birthday?
- ◆ Where were you born?
- ◆ Tell us about your family.
- ◆ Do you have siblings? How many? What are their names?
- ◆ Describe your personality and physical appearance. What are you like?

Professional Development ◆ 235

- ◆ What classes do you have? How many? When?
- ◆ What did you do last summer?
- ◆ Which languages do you speak?
- ◆ Describe your daily routine.
- ◆ Where do you like to go shopping?
- ◆ Do you play sports?
- ◆ What is your favorite movie?
- ◆ What is your favorite food?
- ◆ Describe the typical foods of your country.
- ◆ What is your favorite TV show?
- ◆ What are your favorite hobbies?
- ◆ What do you do on weekends?
- ◆ Shopping: describe how it is done in your community.
- ◆ Sports: describe some popular sports in your country. Which ones do you like?
- ◆ Describe your daily routine.
- ◆ What is your house like?
- ◆ Describe your city.
- ◆ What do you do during the holidays?

These are some simple questions for Novice learners. I learn these simple questions and how to answer them (learning). The real payoff lies in the responses of the other speaker, where a learner can acquire language through their responses. Create questions based on what you need to learn to talk about in your target language.

Learning new languages is a strong personal interest. A surprising benefit of learning languages other than the ones that one teaches is that they allow us to see languages through a learner's lens. If you do this activity in the language that you do teach, a recording serves as a great listening activity for your students.

#7: Study Abroad

I love attending language schools abroad. I make fast progress and feel like I'm on vacation at the same time. There are ways to get the cash to afford it.

The first way would be to give lessons on a site like italki. You could also do a side hustle by teaching English on a site like VIP Kids.

If those things don't fill your cup, there are some other ways. Some years ago, Farnoosh Torabi introduced me to the idea of Chase's cash-back reward cards. You could earn points on a reward, a travel reward card, which of course would help you travel and study abroad, but you could also earn points for cash back by shopping for things like your gas or your groceries. Whatever you need and whatever your monthly expenses are, put it on your credit card and pay it off every month (important). This could allow you to fund a trip abroad.

I once spent five weeks at an Airbnb in Paris. You have your own place? You could Airbnb your place out and use rewards, completely funding your stay with your side hustle and rewards money. You could also consider teaching abroad. It might not offer you a lot of free time to practice languages, but you could travel and earn a bit of money. You could also volunteer abroad. There are programs for hosting exchange students as well.

#8: Train in Language Proficiency Rating

One of the most valuable pieces of professional development was earning certification with the Center for Applied Linguistics on rating language proficiency tests. While the ACTFL/LTI OPI rater training is perhaps more comprehensive, teachers might need support from their institution to obtain their certification and maintain it. The CAL rater training was perfect to learn to rate language proficiency at an affordable price. There was no travel to consider either (as much fun as that is). The combination of going through the proficiency levels as a learner and then doing the training provided a solid foundation to provide experiences for learners to reach any level of proficiency they desire.

Don't Reinvent the Wheel, and Find Your Peeps

I *so* wish social media had been where it is today when I first started teaching.

I love all these teachers on Facebook and Instagram sharing their classrooms and their ideas, and offering one another support. Do a quick Instagram search and find some people who teach your language, as well as teachers who teach other languages. They will be an invaluable source of support, inspiration, and ideas.

While Pinterest is a great place to plan a wedding or a party, or find recipes, it offers so much more than that. It's a search engine, a place to find and save your ideas, find inspiration, see other classrooms, and get professional development. I find that this is one of my most valuable resources for teaching languages.

The teachers contributing their brilliant activities to this project have loads of great ideas for the language classroom:

Amy Marshall, Zona de Profes
Spanish with Stephanie, spanishwithstephanie.com
Kate Clifton, katelanguages.co.uk
Dr. Emilia Illana Mahiques, Cornell University
Andrea Nazelli, Spanish teacher
Gretchen Burke, Spanish teacher
Rita Jimenez, Spanish teacher
Dr. Stephanie Knouse, Furman University
Dr. Begoña Caballero-García, Wofford College

I am so appreciative of your spending this time with me sharing how to build proficiency in world language learners. I share videos and podcasts on my blog https://reallifelanguage.com/reallifelanguageblog, as well as on YouTube, Pinterest, and Instagram. Please stop by and say hello.